#OPERATIONSOCKDRAWER

the knitmore girls

operation
SOCk
drawer

THE GUIDE TO BUILDING YOUR
STASH OF HAND-KNIT SOCKS

Interweave

Heartfelt thanks to Hayley DeBerard, Allison Korleski,
Andrea Lotz & Jenn Rein for modeling!

 Interweave®
An imprint of Penguin Random House LLC
penguinrandomhouse.com

10 9 8 7 6 5 4 3 2 1
ISBN-13: 978-1-63250-696-2

Editorial Director Kerry Bogert

Editors Nathalie Mornu & Kerry Bogert

Technical Editor Kate Atherley

Cover & Interior Designer pnormandesigns

Photographer Harper Point Photography

contents

introduction

**BY JASMIN & GIGI,
THE KNITMORE GIRLS**

IT STARTED WITH two worsted-weight skeins of hand-painted yarn: one zebra striped, the other brightly variegated and rainbow colored, sold with the Cottage Creations booklet (the one from the early 1990s, the ubiquitous one with the sock recipe). It was the usual fiber festival scene: knitters and crocheters gathered in a huge convention center, colorful skeins of yarn as far as the eye could see, wool fumes in abundance. Gigi bought a kit, brought it home, and made Jasmin a pair of socks. And then another. And then another.

> Socks are the bonbon of the knitting world: a small, decadent bite. You can carry one in-progress around in your purse, stash it on the dashboard of your car, or—for the bold of heart and firm of bottom—behind the cushions of your couch.

Jasmin wore them cheerfully with her super-cool Birkenstock sandals. When Jasmin got really into spinning her own yarn, Gigi agreed to knit socks out of any yarn she spun. It was a pretty terrific arrangement.

Not long after, Jasmin started knitting socks, too. She used different yarn and learned from a different book and—despite Gigi's expertise—dug in her heels and informed her mom that she didn't need any help. (Jasmin was 14.) Those socks turned out lovely, and it was a great lesson in using the right yarn for the right project. (100% alpaca socks are divinely decadent, but they lacked the necessary elasticity. They make a great slouchy sock, though.)

Socks are the bonbon of the knitting world: a small, decadent bite. You can carry one in-progress around in your purse, stash it on the dashboard of your car, or—for the bold of heart and firm of bottom—behind the cushions of your couch. (This last one violates Rule #2 in Gigi's Rules of Knitting, though: *Never Leave Your Knitting on a Chair*. Rule #1, naturally, is *Always Finish Your Row*.)

Because you're holding this book, we know you're a sock knitter. If our observations are correct, we'd even guess that when you bought the yarn for your first pair of socks, you probably bought yarn for **at least** two pairs—before you even knew you liked knitting socks! That's how irresistible sock knitting is. It's really the yarn; it's always the yarn. Whether it's a rich semisolid, a bold variegated, or a cheerful self-striping, each skein of sock yarn sings its siren song: Buy me. You want me. Wiggle your toes and imagine me as a pair of socks. See? We're just right for each other. And before you know it, that skein and some of its friends have made their merry way into your stash. How do we know? Because, fellow sock knitters, we are one of you.

Before we can talk about the Etsy incident of 2014, we have to talk about Instagram. Instagram is, by far, the most tempting place for a knitter to go. It's a never-ending stream of gorgeous knitting, irresistible yarn, and so much inspiration. It's also a powerful medium for learning about the lives and experiences of others in our community—the

As Jasmin scrolled through her [Instagram] feed, her knitting life changed. Susan B. Anderson, sock knitter and designer extraordinaire, had posted a picture of her sock drawer . . . it completely changed the way Jasmin looked at knitting socks.

"secret sauce" of the diverse knitting community. In what can feel like a very isolating world (and activity), the people behind the knitting and the yarn take it from "just" a skein of yarn and give the fiber meaning, making it special. Vacation yarn, festival yarn, gift yarn, you-would-not-believe-what-I-paid-for-this-on-sale yarn: each skein has a story. When you compliment a knitter's socks, shawl, sweater, or hat, you'll be hard-pressed not to get the name of the pattern, the person or business who dyed the yarn, and—if it's handspun—sometimes the name of the sheep, too!

You might not know this, but Instagram was actually developed by knitters who understood the need to stand and shout, "I'm knitting this thing, and isn't it amazing?!" from the rooftops. We guess they developed it because they didn't receive an appropriately enthusiastic response from their loved ones when explaining why their knitting was so exciting. (Okay, so this story isn't even remotely true, but Jasmin really wants it to be. After all these years, she showed her spouse a particularly ingenious method of shaping, and he responded with, "Oh.")

"'Oh'? I'm putting this on Instagram. This is more than just 'Oh,'" she told him. Instagram, as usual, did not disappoint.)

As Jasmin scrolled through her feed, her knitting life changed. Susan B. Anderson, sock knitter and designer extraordinaire, had posted a picture of

her sock drawer. On the surface, you might think that's nothing earth-shattering, but it completely changed the way Jasmin looked at knitting socks. The goal was no longer to just knit beautiful socks (just?), but now to knit an entire drawer of heart-stopping, makes-your-heart-sing-they're-so-cheerful, statement socks.

The darker side of inspiration (and admiration) is envy, and Susan's sock drawer brought out Jasmin's inner green-eyed monster. Envy as green as an appropriately named skein of indie-dyed sock yarn. And that's how the Etsy incident of 2014 started, with skeins from dyers from around the world finding their way into Jasmin's cart, then her mailbox, and ultimately, onto Instagram and into her sock drawer.

With a tongue-in-cheek hashtag, Jasmin's trademark enthusiasm, and the camaraderie that comes with a knit-along of epic proportions, we encouraged the listeners of our very popular podcast to follow suit and make their own drawers of beautiful socks. #Operationsockdrawer was off! Our Knitmore Vanilla sock pattern is free on Ravelry (with instructions given exactly as we do it), but this book is for those of you ready for something exciting, a little challenging, and a whole lot cheerful.

We welcome you to join us and the tens of thousands of others knitting their hearts' desires for a bevy of sensational socks and create the sock drawer of your dreams!

MORE THAN 200,000 PHOTOS HAVE
BEEN TAGGED #OPERATIONSOCKDRAWER
SINCE 2014 WHEN JASMIN & GIGI STARTED THEIR
QUEST TO KNIT A DRAWER FULL OF SOCKS AS
INSPIRING AS SUSAN B. ANDERSON'S.

PHOTO: EVAN ANDERSON

rêveurs

— CHERYL EATON —

DESIGNED FOR DREAMERS, Rêveurs features Japanese lace elements inspired by the ethereal ice gardens of the Cirque des Rêves, from the book *The Night Circus*, by Erin Morgenstern. These socks are intended as an identifying symbol for Rêveurs. They begin with an Old Norwegian Cast-On. Twisted 1x1 rib brings to mind striped carnival circus tents. It leads to playful flowing lace, which represents magical blooming ice flowers. Although the Japanese knot stitches look complicated, they're easy to knit and a fun introduction to a new technique. An attractive yet sturdy Eye of Partridge heel flap is perfect for wandering around all those magical attractions! As the pattern moves onto the foot, the lace changes to an easily memorized motif that hugs the foot. You can adjust the length for a perfect fit.

WORKED TOP DOWN, WITH A FLAP-AND-GUSSET HEEL & GRAFTED WEDGE TOE.

Finished Size
XS (S, M, L, XL)

Sock's foot circumference: 7 (7½, 8, 8½, 9)" (18 [19, 20.5, 21.5, 23] cm) to be worn with about 1" (2.5 cm) negative ease.

Yarn
Fingering weight (#1 Super Fine).

Shown here: Hedgehog Fibres Twist Sock (80% Blue Faced Leicester wool, 20% nylon; 399 yd [365 m]/3½ oz [100 g]): Sour Cherry, 1 skein.

Needles
Size U.S. 1 (2.25 mm): Your preferred configuration for small circumference in the round: DPNs, long circular for magic loop, 2 shorter circulars, set of three flexible DPNs, 8-9" (20-23 cm) circular.

Adjust needle size if necessary to obtain correct gauge.

Notions
Stitch marker; yarn needle.

Gauge
34 sts and 50 rnds = 4" (10 cm) in Stockinette st.

29 sts and 32 rnds of Rêveurs Leg patt measure about 4" (10 cm) long and 3½" (9 cm) wide.

Notes
- Needles with sharp tips will really help with the double decreases.

STITCH GUIDE

Knot Stitch: slip third st on left needle over the first two stitches and let drop off the needle; k, yo, k over remaining two sts

Knot Stitch with Left-leaning Decrease: slip next st purlwise. Slip the third st on left needle over the first two stitches and let drop off the needle. Place the first slipped st back onto left needle; ssk, yo, k

Knot Stitch with Right-leaning Decrease: slip the third st on left needle over the first two stitches and let drop off the needle; k, yo, k2tog

socks

Using the Old Norwegian Cast-On method (see Glossary), CO 60 (64, 68, 72, 76) sts. Distribute sts across needles as you prefer and join for working in the round. Note or mark start of round as required.

CUFF

Rnd 1: [K1 tbl, p1] around.

Repeat Rnd 1 as set until cuff measures about 1" (2.5 cm) from the cast-on edge, or desired length.

LEG

Rnd 1: K1 tbl, [p1, k1 tbl] 0 (0, 1, 1, 2) times, p5, [k1 tbl, p1] 9 times, k1 tbl, p5, [k1 tbl, p1] to EOR.

Rnd 2: K1 tbl, [p1, k1 tbl] 0 (0, 1, 1, 2) times, work Rêveurs Leg Chart over next 29 sts, [k1 tbl, p1] 1 (1, 2, 2, 3) times, k to last st of round, p1.

Rêveurs Leg Chart

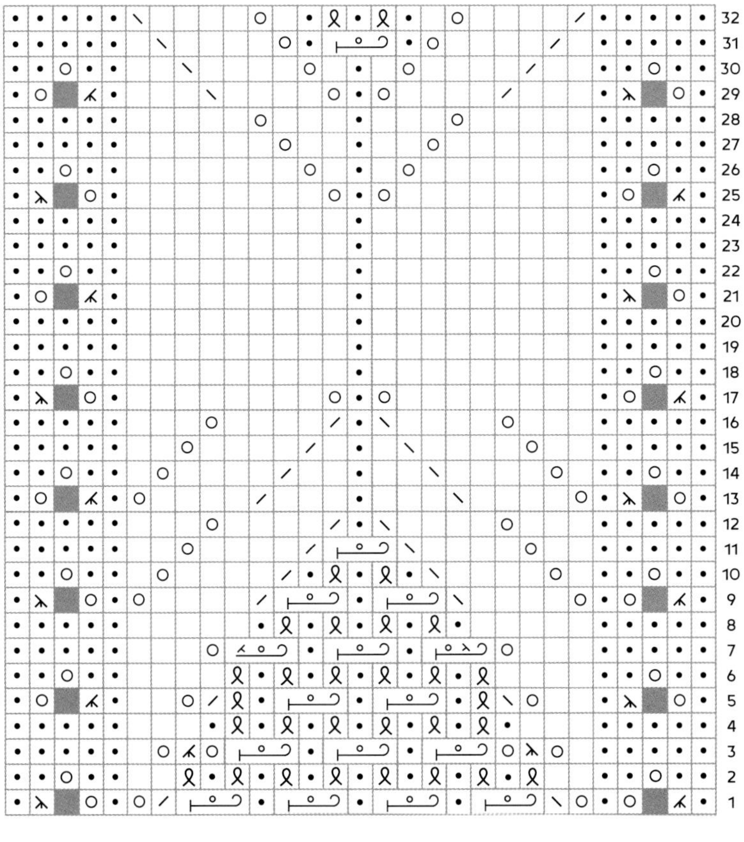

knit
purl
yo
k1 tbl
ssk
k2tog
k3tog
sl1, k2tog, psso
knot stitch*
knot stitch with left-leaning dec*
knot stitch with right-leaning dec*
no stitch
* see stitch guide

Rêveurs Foot Chart

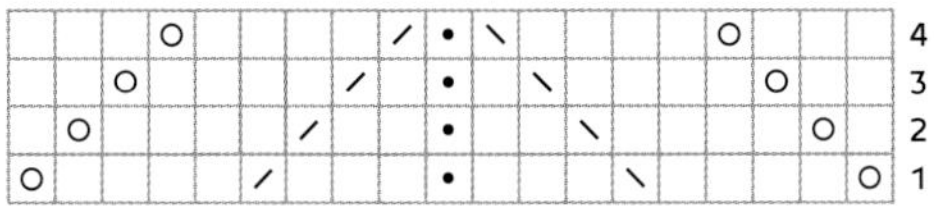

Rnd 2 sets the leg pattern. Work in patt as set until Rêveurs Leg Chart has been completed twice, then work Rnds 1–12 once more (76 rounds worked).

HEEL FLAP

Setup Row: [K1, p1] 1 (0, 1, 0, 1) times, [k1 tbl, p1] 2 (3, 3, 4, 4) times, work 19 sts of Rêveurs Foot Chart, p1, [k1 tbl, p1] 2 (3, 3, 4, 4) times—30 (32, 34, 36, 38) instep sts. These will be held for the instep—slip them to a single needle or holder as desired.

The heel flap will be worked flat across the rem 30 (32, 34, 36, 38) sts.

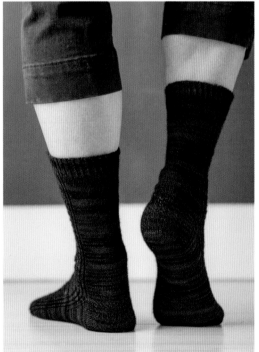

Row 1: (RS) Sl 1 wyb, k3, [sl 1, k1] to last 4 sts, k4.

Row 2: (WS) Sl 1 wyf, k3, p to last 4 sts, k4.

Row 3: Sl 1 wyb, k3, [k1, sl 1] to last 4 sts, k4.

Row 4: Sl 1 wyf, k3, p to last 4 sts, k4.

Repeat these 4 rows 7 (7, 8, 8, 8) more times.

HEEL TURN

Row 1: (RS) Sl 1 wyb, k16 (18, 18, 20, 20), ssk, k1, turn.

Row 2: (WS) Sl 1 wyf, p5 (7, 5, 7, 5), p2tog, p1, turn.

Row 3: Sl 1 wyb, k to 1 st before gap, ssk, k1, turn.

Row 4: Sl 1 wyf, p to 1 st before gap, p2tog, p1, turn.

Repeat Rows 3-4 until all heel sts have been worked, ending after a WS row—18 (20, 20, 22, 22) sts.

GUSSET

Setup Rnd: Sl 1 wyb, k17 (19, 19, 21, 21) heel sts, pick up and knit 17 (17, 19, 19, 19) sts along the edge of the heel flap; [k1, p1] 1 (0, 1, 0, 1) times, [k1 tbl, p1] 2 (3, 3, 4, 4) times, Rêveurs Foot Chart across 19 sts, p1, [k1 tbl, p1] 2 (3, 3, 4, 4) times; pick up and knit 17 (17, 19, 19, 19) sts along the edge of the heel flap, k across heel sts and first set of picked up sts. This is the new EOR; place marker or rearrange sts as you prefer—82 (86, 92, 96, 98) sts.

Dec Rnd: Work in patt as set across instep, k1, ssk, k to 3 sts before EOR, k2tog, k1 (p1, k1, p1, k1)—2 sts dec'd.

Note: For sizes S and L, the last st of the sole is worked as a purl throughout Gusset and Foot.

Following Rnd: Work even in patt as set.

Repeat last two rnds 10 (10, 11, 11, 10) more times—60 (64, 68, 72, 76) sts rem; 30 (32, 34, 36, 38) sts each on instep and sole.

FOOT

Work even in patt as set until foot measures 1¼ (1¼, 1½, 1½, 1½)" (3.2 [3.2, 3.8, 3.8, 3.8] cm) less than desired length from back of heel, ending on Rnd 4.

TOE

Rnd 1: K1, ssk, k to last 2 sts of instep, k2tog, k2, ssk, k to last 3 sts, k2tog, k1—4 sts dec'd.

Rnd 2: Knit.

Repeat Rnds 1 and 2 [4 (4, 5, 5, 5)] more times—40 (44, 44, 48, 52) sts rem.

Repeat Rnd 1 [5 (6, 6, 6, 7)] more times—20 (20, 20, 24, 24) sts rem.

finishing

Cut yarn, leaving a 12" (30 cm) tail. Divide sts evenly across two needles, and with tail threaded on a yarn needle, use Kitchener stitch (see Glossary) to graft toe closed.

To block, simply wash the socks. Weave in ends once dry.

churfirsten

— SABRINA SCHUMACHER —

CHURFIRSTEN IS A mountain range in the canton of St. Gallen, Switzerland, with seven peaks of remarkably uniform heights. Inspired by the views in this region, knit and purl peaks are formed over the leg and foot of these wonderfully textured socks. The stitch pattern reveals itself depending on the angle of light and shows best with solid, semisolid, and lightly speckled yarn. Starting with a flexible cast-on, the twisted ribbing flows into the triangle pattern. The vertical seam on the back of the calf gives the leg elasticity, allowing the fit to accommodate different sizes. This vertical seam increases to a triangle that forms the heel and is worked in reverse Stockinette stitch.

WORKED TOP DOWN, WITH AN INTEGRATED-GUSSET STRONG HEEL & GRAFTED WEDGE TOE.

Finished Size

XS (S, M, L, XL)

Sock's foot circumference: 6½ (7, 7⅛, 8, 8½)" (16.5 [18, 19, 20.5, 21.5] cm) to be worn with about 1" (2.5 cm) negative ease.

Yarn

Fingering weight (#1 Super Fine).

Shown here: Penny Lane Yarns Foot Lane (75% superwash Merino, 25% polyamide; 465 yd [425 m]/3½ oz [100 g]): Ruby, 1 skein.

Needles

Size U.S. 1½ (2.5 mm): Your preferred configuration for small circumference in the round: DPNs, long circular for magic loop, 2 shorter circulars, set of three flexible DPNs, 8–9" (20–23 cm) circular.

Adjust needle size if necessary to obtain the correct gauge.

Notions

2 stitch markers; yarn needle.

Gauge

32 sts and 48 rnds = 4" (10 cm) in Stockinette st.

socks

Using your preferred stretchy method, CO 52 (56, 60, 64, 68) sts. Distribute sts across needles as you prefer and join for working in the round. Note or mark start of round as required.

CUFF

Sizes XS, M, XL Only

Rnd 1: P1, [k1 tbl, p2, k1 tbl, p1, k1 tbl, p2] 6 (-, 7, -, 8) times, k1 tbl, p2.

Repeat the last rnd 15 more times.

Rnd 17: P1, k1 tbl, k to last 3 sts, k1 tbl, p2.

Sizes S, L Only

Rnd 1: P1, k1 tbl, p1, [k1 tbl, p2, k1 tbl, p1, k1 tbl, p2] - (6, -, 7, -) times, k1 tbl, p1, k1 tbl, p2.

Repeat the last rnd 15 more times.

Rnd 17: [p1, k1 tbl] 2 times, k to last 5 sts, k1 tbl, p1, k1 tbl, p2.

LEG

All Sizes

Rnd 1: [P1, k1 tbl] 1 (2, 1, 2, 1) times, work across Churfirsten Leg Chart to last 3 (5, 3, 5, 3) sts.

Cont as set until you have worked the 16 rnds of Churfirsten Leg Chart 3 (4, 4, 4, 5) times, and cont until you have completed Rnd 12 (10, 8, 6, 4) of the next repeat.

Note: If you want to shorten or lengthen the regular calf length, work Rnds 1–16 once less or more, before the final rnds.

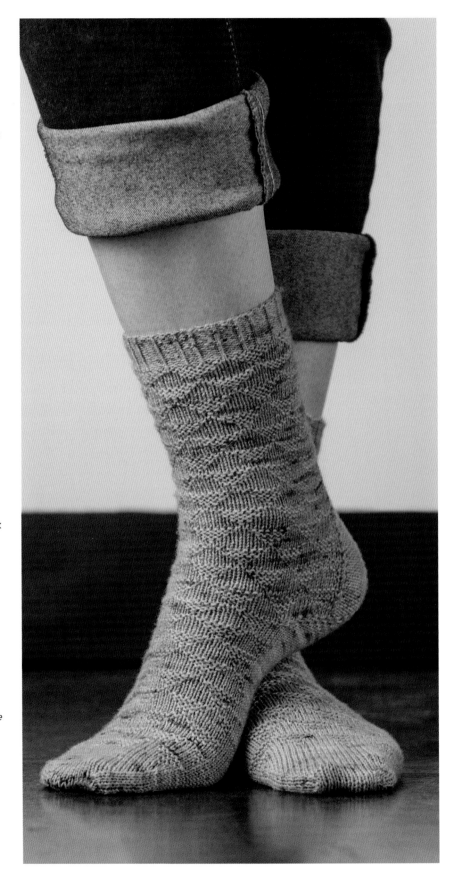

HEEL

Sizes XS, M, XL Only

Rnd 1: P1, M1p, pm, k1 tbl, work in patt as set to last 3 sts, k1 tbl, pm, M1p, p to end—2 sts inc'd.

Rnd 2: P to m, sm, k1 tbl, k to 1 st before m, k1 tbl, sm, p to end.

Repeat the last 2 rnds 12 (–, 14, –, 16) more times—78 (–, 90, –, 102) sts.

Next rnd: P to m, remove m, k1 tbl, work in established Leg patt over 10 (–, 12, –, 14) sts, pm, work in established leg patt over 27 (–, 31, –, 35) sts, pm, work across leg patt as set to 1 (–, 1, –, 1) sts before m, k1 tbl, remove m, p to last 5 sts, k5.

Sizes S, L Only

Rnd 1: P1, M1p, pm, k1 tbl, p1, k1 tbl, work in patt as set to last 5 sts, k1 tbl, p1, k1 tbl, pm, M1p, p to end—2 sts inc'd.

Rnd 2: P to m, sm, k1 tbl, p1, k1 tbl, k to 3 sts before m, k1 tbl, p1, k1 tbl, sm, p to end.

Repeat the last 2 rnds – (13, –, 15, –) more times— – (84, –, 96, –) sts.

Next rnd: P to m, remove m, k1 tbl, p1, k1 tbl, work in established leg patt over – (9, –, 11, –) sts, pm, work in established leg patt over – (29, –, 33, –) sts, pm, work across leg patt as set to – (3, –, 3, –) sts before m, k1 tbl, p1, k1 tbl, remove m, p to last 5 sts, k5—27 (29, 31, 33, 35) instep sts between the markers; 51 (55, 59, 63, 67) heel sts; 78 (84, 90, 96, 102) total sts.

> **Note:** You are positioned in the center of the heel.

Churfirsten Leg Chart

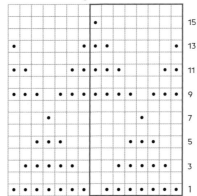

- ☐ knit
- ⊡ purl
- ☐ pattern repeat

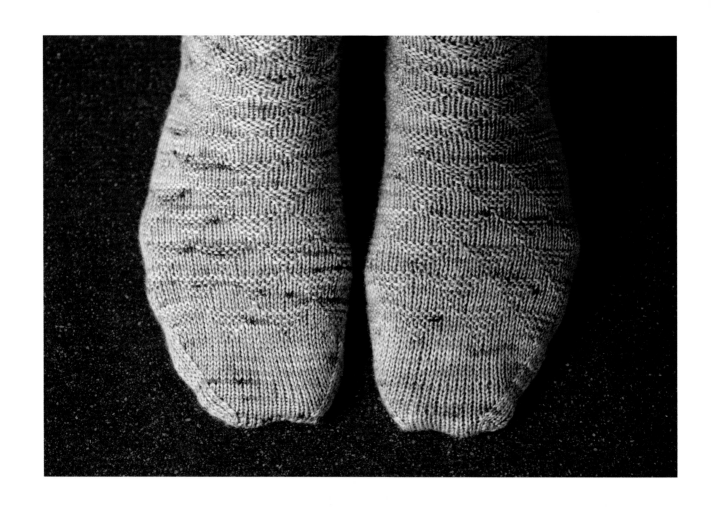

Churfirsten Instep Chart

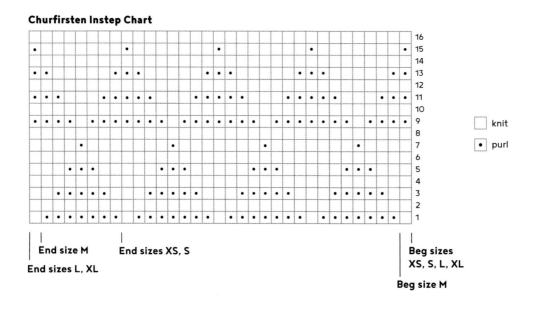

knit

• purl

End size M

End sizes L, XL

End sizes XS, S

Beg sizes
XS, S, L, XL

Beg size M

TURN HEEL

Row 1: (RS) K3, ssk, k1, turn.

Row 2: (WS) Sl 1 wyf, p8, p2tog, p1, turn.

Row 3: Sl 1 wyb, k to 1 st before gap, ssk, k1, turn.

Row 4: Sl 1 wyf, p to 1 st before gap, p2tog, p1, turn.

Repeat Rows 3 and 4 [7 (8, 9, 10, 11)] more times—3 sts rem unworked on either side of the heel.

Row 5: Sl 1 wyb, k to 1 st before gap, ssk, turn.

Row 6: Sl 1 wyf, p to 1 st before gap, p2tog, turn.

Rows 7–8: Repeat last 2 rows once more—56 (60, 64, 68, 72) sts.

Row 9: Sl 1 wyb, 1, k to 1 st before gap, ssk. Do not turn.

Resume working in rnds as foll:

Next rnd: K across instep, k2tog, k to end—54 (58, 62, 66, 70) sts; 27 (29, 31, 33, 35) each on instep and sole.

FOOT

Sizes XS, S, M, L Only

Rnd 1: K1 (2, 0, 0, –), work Churfirsten Instep Chart Rnd 1 starting and ending at st indicated for your size, k to end.

Rnd 2: K to end.

Size XL Only

Rnd 1: K1, work Instep Chart Rnd 9 starting and ending at st indicated for size XL, k to end.

Rnd 2: K to end.

All Sizes

Cont in established patt and work until piece measures 1½ (1¾, 1¾, 2, 2)" (3.8 [4.5, 4.5, 5, 5] cm) less than desired finished sock foot length, ending with an odd rnd of Churfirsten Instep Chart.

TOE

Dec Rnd: K1, ssk, k to 3 sts before end of instep, k2tog, k2, ssk, k to last 3 sts, k2tog, k1—4 sts decreased.

Next Rnd: Knit.

Repeat last 2 rnds 8 (9, 9, 10, 10) more times—18 (18, 22, 22, 26) sts rem.

finishing

Cut yarn, leaving a 12" (30 cm) tail. Divide sts evenly across two needles, and with tail threaded on a yarn needle, use Kitchener stitch (see Glossary) to graft toe closed.

To block, simply wash the socks. Weave in ends once dry.

ABOUT THE DESIGNER

Sabrina Schumacher is a passionate knitter and designer from Switzerland. Her design style focuses primarily on texture, color, and geometric patterns. Inspired by nature and architecture, her patterns are usually named after places she knows from kite surfing and paragliding.

THE BEAUTIFUL GEOMETRIC shapes and colors of stained glass inspired these gorgeous ankle socks. Using two contrasting colors of yarn—one a solid color and the other a variegated color yarn—for the stranded colorwork detail creates a lovely effect. The molded frames holding dappled panes of "glass" are achieved with the dark, rich, solid color yarn, while the heavily speckled, variegated yarn creates the central glass portion. The stained glass stranded colorwork detail is worked for the instep portion of the sock, with the heel, bottom, and toe worked in the solid color yarn. Each Stained Glass sock is one-of-a-kind when using a variegated yarn because of the strong variation of color throughout the skein. This uniqueness makes for particularly fun knitting!

WORKED TOP DOWN, WITH A FLAP-AND-GUSSET HEEL & GRAFTED WEDGE TOE.

Finished Size

XS (S, M, L, XL)

Sock's foot circumference: 6 (7, 8, 9, 10)" (15 [18, 20.5, 23, 25.5] cm) to be worn with about ½" (1.5 cm) negative ease.

Yarn

Fingering weight (#1 Super Fine).

Shown here: Spun Right Round Classic Sock (100% superwash Merino; 438 yd [401 m]/3½ oz [100 g]): (MC) Reaper's Rags, (CC) Pack Your Maniac, 1 skein each.

Needles

Size U.S. 1½ (2.5 mm): Your preferred configuration for small circumference in the round: DPNs, long circular for magic loop, 2 shorter circulars, set of three flexible DPNs, 8-9" (20-23 cm) circular.

Adjust needle size if necessary to obtain the correct gauge.

Notions

Stitch markers; yarn needle.

Gauge

32 sts and 40 rnds = 4" (10 cm) in Stockinette st.

36 sts and 48 rnds = 4" (10 cm) in Stained Glass Chart patt.

Notes

■ This fabric has less stretch than Stockinette, and for comfort, the socks need to be a little larger than for plain fabric.

■ For the foot section, make sure to carry the contrasting color along with the main color in the sole of the sock, and trap/catch the floats every second stitch. To do this, place the nonworking yarn over the right needle's tip, then knit the next stitch. The nonworking yarn can be moved back down so that when the next stitch is knit, it catches the nonworking yarn.

stained glass

— FIONA MUNRO FROM
MUNRO SISTERS 3 —

socks

With MC, CO 48 (56, 64, 72, 80) sts. Distribute sts across needles as you prefer and join for working in the rnd. Note or mark start of rnd as required.

CUFF

Ribbing Rnd: [K1, p1] around.

Work ribbing as set for ½" (1.5 cm).

LEG

Join CC.

Leg Rnd: Work Stained Glass Chart around.

Work as set through Row 8 of the chart.

HEEL FLAP

The heel is worked in MC only on the first 24 (28, 32, 36, 40) sts. Do not cut CC.

Row 1: (RS) Sl 1 wyb, k23 (27, 31, 35, 39), turn.

Row 2: (WS) Sl 1 wyf, p23 (27, 31, 35, 39), turn.

Repeat the last 2 rows 11 (13, 15, 17, 19) more times.

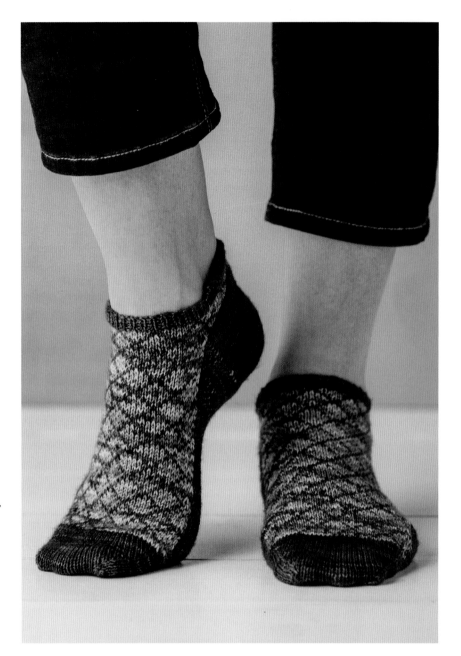

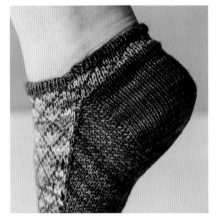

Stained Glass Chart

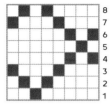

8-st patt rep

■ MC □ CC

HEEL TURN

Row 1: (RS) K14 (16, 19, 21, 23), ssk, k1, turn.

Row 2: (WS) Sl 1 wyf, p5 (5, 7, 7, 7), p2tog, p1, turn.

Row 3: Sl 1 wyb, k to 1 st before gap, ssk, k1, turn.

Row 4: Sl 1 wyf, p to 1 st before gap, p2tog, p1, turn.

Repeat Rows 3 and 4 [3 (3, 4, 5, 6)] more times—14 (18, 20, 22, 26) sts.

Sizes XS, S Only

Row 5: Sl 1 wyb, k to 1 st before gap, ssk, turn.

Row 6: Sl 1 wyf, p to 1 st before gap, p2tog—14 (16, -, -, -) sts.

GUSSET

With MC, k14 (16, 20, 22, 24) heel sts, pick up and knit 12 (14, 16, 18, 20) sts along the edge of the heel flap, work Stained Glass patt as set for 24 (28, 32, 36, 40) sts starting with st 1 (5, 1, 5, 1) of the chart; working with MC but carrying CC in the back, pick up and knit 12 (14, 16, 18, 20) sts along the edge of the heel flap—62 (72, 84, 94, 104) sts.

> **Note:** As you work the foot, carry the CC along the sole, trapping the floats every 2 sts.

Dec Rnd: K to 2 sts before instep, k2tog, work instep in patt as set; ssk, k to EOR—2 sts dec'd.

Next Rnd: Work even in patt as set.

Repeat the last 2 rnds 6 (7, 9, 10, 11) more times—48 (56, 64, 72, 80) sts.

FOOT

Maintain Stained Glass Chart patt as set across instep sts and sole sts in MC, knitting all rnds until sock measures 1¾ (2, 2, 2, 2)" (4.5 [5, 5, 5, 5] cm) short of desired foot length, ending final rnd at start of instep sts.

Cut CC.

TOE

Rnd 1: K1, ssk, k to 3 sts before end of instep, k2tog, k2, ssk, k to 3 sts before EOR, k2tog, k1—4 sts dec'd.

Rnd 2: Knit.

Repeat the last 2 rnds until 12 (12, 20, 28, 36) sts rem.

finishing

Cut yarn, leaving a 12" (30 cm) tail. Divide sts evenly across two needles, and with tail threaded on a yarn needle, use Kitchener stitch (see Glossary) to graft toe closed.

To block, simply wash the socks. Weave in ends once dry.

meta

— MARY HULL —

WHAT SOCK KNITTER doesn't have a stash of leftover bits of sock yarn? The Meta sock takes advantage of those, with extra scraps taking on a whole new life and serving as reminders of past projects. This pattern can serve as a tactile holder for beloved memories. What story will your socks tell? Each band of color requires about 4 yards (3.6 m). Play with color and dye lots; this sock can handle about any dye technique as long as the main color retreats into the background. Don't be terrified at the thought of all those ends—the pattern calls for minimal finishing!

WORKED TOP DOWN, WITH A FLAP-AND-GUSSET HEEL & GRAFTED WEDGE TOE.

Finished Size
XS (S, M, L, XL)

Sock's foot circumference: 7 (7½, 8, 8½, 9)" (18 [19, 20.5, 21.5, 23] cm) to be worn with about 1" (2.5 cm) negative ease.

Yarn
Fingering weight (#1 Super Fine).

Shown here: MC: Sun Valley Fibers MCN-F (80% Merino, 10% cashmere, 10% nylon; 400 yd [366 m]/3½ oz [100 g]: Kensington, 1 skein.
CCs (required 4 yd [3.6 m] per stripe):

1 | BlueberryChickYarn Kiawah (75% superwash Merino, 25% nylon; 463 yd [423 m]/3½ oz [100 g]): Beautyberry.

2 | Lofty Loops Yarns Lofty Sock (80% superwash Merino, 20% nylon; 400 yd [366 m]/3½ oz [100 g]): 700 Jumps Ain't Healthy Boy.

3 | Unwind Yarn Company Honeymoon Sock (100% superwash Merino; 430 yd [393 m]/3½ oz [100 g]): Meyer Lemon.

4 | Teal fingering weight superwash Merino-silk blend sock yarn.

5 | Lilliput Yarn Simple Sock (80% superwash Merino; 20% nylon; 400 yd [365 m]/3½ oz [100 g]): Gracie.

6 | Cowgirlblues Merino Sock (100% Merino; 164 yd [150 m]/1¾ oz [50 g]): Ruby Grapefruit.

7 | Unwind Yarn Company Twinkle Sock (75% superwash Merino, 20% nylon, 5% stellina; 438 yd [400 m]/3½ oz [100 g]): Lake Frances Sunrise.

8 | The Fiber Seed Sprout Sock (90% Merino, 10% nylon; 510 yd [466 m]/4¾ oz [135 g]): Birch.

9 | BlueberryChickYarn Kiawah (75% superwash Merino, 25% nylon; 460 yd [421 m]/3½ oz [100 g]): Wheat Field.

10 | Marigoldjen Superwash Merino Nylon Sock (75% superwash Merino, 25% nylon; 460 yd [421 m]/3½ oz [100 g]): Odette.

11 | Sweet Paprika Designs Allegretto (70% Merino, 20% bamboo, 10% nylon; 410 yd [375 m]/4 oz [115 g]): Aurora.

12 | Sweet Paprika Designs Allegretto (70% Merino, 20% bamboo, 10% nylon; 410 yd [375 m]/4 oz [115 g]): Glacier.

Needles
Size U.S. 1 (2.25 mm): Your preferred configuration for small circumference in the round: DPNs, long circular for magic loop, 2 shorter circulars, set of three flexible DPNs, 8-9" (20-23 cm) circular.

Adjust needle size if necessary to obtain the correct gauge.

Notions
Yarn needle.

Gauge
34 sts and 46 rnds = 4" (10 cm) in Stockinette st.

31 sts and 64 rnds = 4" (10 cm) in st patt.

STITCH GUIDE
CC: Patt uses MC to designate the main color, and CC for the contrast color stripes. Pick a different color to use as the CC for each stripe.

K4B: Insert right needle into st 4 rnds below the next st on the left needle. (This will be the last MC st below the next st on the left needle.) Carefully drop all the sts down to that spot and knit through that st as you normally would.

socks
With MC, CO 56 (60, 64, 68, 72) sts. Distribute sts across needles as you prefer and join for working in the round. Note or mark start of round as required.

CUFF
Rnd 1: [K1, p1] around.

Repeat Rnd 1 until ribbing measures 1" (2.5 cm) or desired cuff length.

LEG
Setup Rnd: (MC) K to last 2 sts, k2tog—55 (59, 63, 67, 71) total sts. The first 27 (29, 31, 33, 35) sts form the instep/front of leg; the rem 28 (30, 32, 34, 36) form the heel/sole/back of leg. Place a marker or rearrange sts as you prefer to keep track of the two sets of sts.

Rnd 1: (CC) Knit.

Rnd 2: (CC) Sl 1 wyb, k to end of instep sts, p to EOR.

Rnd 3: (CC) Knit.

Rnd 4: (CC) K across instep sts, p to EOR.

Rnd 5: (MC) K1 (2, 1, 2, 1), [k4b (see Stitch Guide), k3] 6 (6, 7, 7, 8) times, k4b, k to EOR.

Rnd 6: (MC) Sl 1 wyb, k26 (28, 30, 32, 34), p to EOR.

Change to a different CC.

Rnds 7–10: Repeat Rnds 1–4.

Rnd 11: (MC) K3 (4, 3, 4, 3), [k4b, k3] 5 (5, 6, 6, 7) times, k4b, k to EOR.

Rnd 12: (MC) Repeat Rnd 6.

Repeat Rnds 1–12 until leg is desired length, ending last repeat on Rnd 10.

HEEL FLAP

With MC work heel flap as foll:

Setup Rnd: K3 (4, 3, 4, 3), [k4B, k3] 5 (5, 6, 6, 7) times, k4b, k3 (4, 3, 4, 3). The 27 (29, 31, 33, 35) sts just worked will be held to instep; sl to holder or group on a single needle. K to EOR. Heel flap is worked on last 28 (30, 32, 34, 36) sts of rnd.

Row 1: (WS) Sl 1 wyf, p27 (29, 31, 33, 35).

Row 2: (RS) [Sl 1 wyb, k1] 14 (15, 16, 17, 18) times.

Repeat Rows 1 and 2 [12 (13, 14, 15, 16)] times, then work Row 1 once more.

HEEL TURN

Row 1: (RS) Sl 1 wyb, k14 (16, 16, 18, 18), ssk, k1, turn.

Row 2: (WS) Sl 1 wyf, p3 (5, 3, 5, 3), p2tog, p1, turn.

Row 3: Sl 1 wyb, k to 1 st before gap left by turn, ssk, k1, turn.

Row 4: Sl 1 wyf, p to 1 st before gap left by turn, p2tog, p1, turn.

Repeat Rows 3 and 4 until all heel sts have been worked—16 (18, 18, 20, 20) sts rem on heel.

managing many ends

The biggest challenge of the Meta socks is managing all those ends. The following technique will minimize the number of ends to weave in, as well as avoid holes at color changes.

When starting a new CC:

1 | Before starting a new CC, stop 1 st before the end of the previous MC rnd.

2 | Lay the new CC across the MC working yarn **(Fig. 1)** and work the last st of the MC rnd; this traps the new CC under the ladder between the next-to-last and last st of the MC rnd **(Fig. 2)**.

3 | Start CC rnd by working the first st with just the end of the CC attached to the ball of yarn **(Fig. 3)**.

4 | Work the next 3–5 sts by holding the CC working yarn and CC tail together **(Fig. 4)**.

5 | Drop tail and cont working section with CC working yarn **(Fig. 5)**.

When you've finished working with a CC:

1 | Complete the CC section as written. Cut CC yarn, leaving about a 4" (10 cm) tail.

2 | On the next MC rnd, trap the CC yarn to the back of the work as if trapping floats in stranded colorwork. Do this for 8–10 sts, then drop the CC yarn.

3 | Cont working section with MC yarn.

At the end, cut all CC tails, leaving about ¼" (6 mm) on the inside of the sock **(Figs. 6 and 7)**. This will keep the tails from unraveling, and as the socks are worn, those short tails will likely felt into the inside of the sock.

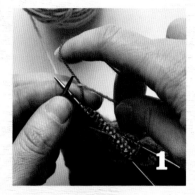

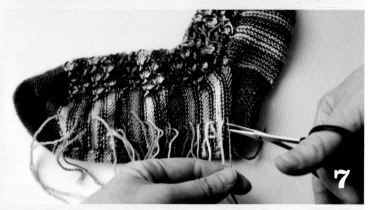

GUSSET

Setup Rnd: (MC) Sl 1 wyb, k15 (17, 17, 19, 19), pick up and knit 15 (16, 17, 18, 19) sts along first edge of heel flap, k27 (29, 31, 33, 35) sts across instep—this corresponds to Rnd 12 of the st patt—pick up and knit 1 st into the corner between the heel flap and instep, pick up and knit 15 (16, 17, 18, 19) sts along second edge of the heel flap, k8 (9, 9, 10, 10). This is the new EOR; pm or rearrange sts as you prefer—72 (79, 83, 89, 93) sts.

Dec Rnd 1: (CC) K to 3 sts before instep, k2tog, k1, k across instep, k1, ssk, k to EOR—2 sts dec'd.

Rnd 2: (CC) Sl 1 wyb, k to end.

Dec Rnd 3: (CC) Repeat Dec Rnd 1.

Rnd 4: (CC) Knit.

Dec Rnd 5: (MC) K to 3 sts before instep, k2tog, k1, k1 (2, 1, 2, 1), [k4b, k3] 6 (6, 7, 7, 8) times, k4b, k1 (2, 1, 2, 1), k1, ssk, k to end—2 sts dec'd.

Rnd 6: (MC) Sl 1 wyb, k to end.

Rnds 7-10: Repeat Rnds 1-4, but with a different CC.

Dec Rnd 11: (MC) K to 3 sts before instep, k2tog, k3 (4, 3, 4, 3), [k4b, k3] 5 (5, 6, 6,7) times, k4b, k3 (4, 3, 4, 3), k1, ssk, k to end—2 sts dec'd.

Rnd 12: (MC) Repeat Rnd 6.

Repeat Gusset Rnds 1-12 until 55 (59, 63, 67, 71) sts rem. Note which rnd you ended on, and then start on the next numbered rnd in the Foot section below. For example, if you ended on Dec Rnd 5 of the Gusset rnds, start with Rnd 6 of the Foot below.

FOOT

Rnd 1: (CC) Knit.

Rnd 2: (CC) Sl 1 wyb, k to end.

Rnds 3-4: (CC) Knit.

Rnd 5: (MC) K to instep, k1 (2, 1, 2, 1), [k4b, k3] 6 (6, 7, 7, 8) times, k4b, k to end.

Rnd 6: (MC) Sl 1 wyb, k to end.

Change to a different CC.

Rnds 7-10: Repeat Rnds 1-4.

Rnd 11: (MC) K to instep, k3 (4, 3, 4, 3), [k4b, k3] 5 (5, 6, 6,7) times, k4b, k to end.

Rnd 12: (MC) Repeat Rnd 6.

Work until foot is approximately 1½ (1½, 1¾, 2, 2)" (4 [4, 4.5, 5, 5] cm) less than desired length, ending on Rnd 6 or 12.

TOE

Work with MC.

Setup Rnd: K to last 2 sts, k2tog—54 (58, 62, 66, 70) sts.

Rnd 1: K to 3 sts before instep, k2tog, k2, ssk, k to last 3 sts of instep, k2tog, k2, ssk, k to end—4 sts dec'd.

Rnd 2: Knit.

Repeat Rnds 1 and 2 until 26 total sts remain, ending with Rnd 1.

Set up for closure: K7.

finishing

Cut yarn, leaving a 12" (30 cm) tail. Divide sts evenly across two needles, and with tail threaded on a yarn needle, use Kitchener stitch (see Glossary) to graft toe closed.

To block, simply wash the socks. Weave in ends once dry.

funhouse

— LISA K. ROSS —

THIS EYE-CATCHING accessory combines stranded colorwork with self-striping yarn for an optical illusion that will keep your attention. Grounded by a solid cuff, heel, and toe, the graphic design calls to mind the reflective mirrors of a funhouse, making these socks as exciting to knit as they are to wear. Concentric diamonds work their way down the front of the sock, with their colors inverted for the back of the leg and the sole. The gusset is worked along the bottom of the heel, creating additional visual interest. This unique footwear looks great from every angle! There's no need to leave home for entertainment when you have your very own Funhouse.

WORKED TOP DOWN, WITH A FLAP-AND-GUSSET HEEL & GRAFTED WEDGE TOE.

Finished Size
S (M, L)

Sock's foot circumference: 8 (9, 10)" (20.5 [23, 25.5] cm).

This fabric has significantly less stretch than Stockinette, and for comfort, the socks need to be a little larger than for plain fabric. Choose a size closest to your actual measurement.

Yarn
Fingering weight (#1 Super Fine).

Shown here: Fab Funky Fibres Hand-Dyed Sock (75% superwash Merino, 25% nylon; 464 yd [424 m]/3½ oz [100 g]): (MC) Silver, and (CC) Falling Leaves, 1 skein each.

Needles
Size U.S. 1 (2.25 mm): Your preferred configuration for small circumference in the round: DPNs, long circular for magic loop, 2 shorter circulars, set of three flexible DPNs, 8-9" (20-23 cm) circular.

Size U.S. 2 (2.75 mm): Your preferred configuration for small circumference in the round: DPNs, long circular for magic loop, 2 shorter circulars, set of three flexible DPNs, 8-9" (20-23 cm) circular.

Adjust needle size if necessary to obtain the correct gauge.

Notions
2 stitch markers; yarn needle.

Gauge
32 sts and 48 rnds = 4" (10 cm) in Stockinette st on smaller needles.

32 sts and 32 rnds = 4" (10 cm) in colorwork patt on larger needles.

Notes

- Be sure to choose yarns with high contrast and no similar colors between the two yarns. If there is any overlap in colors, the design will become muddled.
- When working stranded colorwork, one color will be dominant, meaning that the stitches are slightly larger and this color will be more prominent. In this design, you can choose either color to be dominant, but the important thing is to be consistent. To do this, make a note of how each color is held and be sure that the position of the yarns remains the same throughout the socks.

socks

With smaller needles and MC, CO
56 (64, 72) sts. Distribute sts across
needles as you prefer and join for working in the round. Note or mark start of
round as required.

CUFF

Row 1: [K2, p2] around.

Work ribbing as set until cuff measures
1½" (4 cm) from CO edge. Do not break
yarn.

Inc Rnd: *M1L, k7 (8, 9); rep from * to
EOR—8 sts inc'd; 64 (72, 80) sts.

LEG

Switch to larger needles. Join CC. Work
Funhouse Chart for your size around,
beginning at the bottom right corner of
Row 1. Divide sts or pm at the midpoint
of the rnd to indicate beginning of
instep. Cont in patt until sock leg
measures desired length, ending after
Row 20 of chart.

HEEL FLAP

Switch to smaller needles. You will now
be working with the first half of the
sts and decreasing to the Stockinette
gauge. Arrange the first 32 (36, 40) sts
so they are all on one needle.

> **Note:** The other sts will not be used
> until the gusset is worked. Use MC
> throughout the heel flap and turn. Do
> not break the yarn for the CC.

Dec Row: (RS) With MC, k3 (3, 4), [k2tog,
k6 (7, 8)] 3 times, k2tog, k3 (4, 4)—28
(32, 36) heel sts.

Funhouse Chart, Size S

Funhouse Chart, Size M

MC ☐ CC ■ gusset placement ☐

Funhouse Chart, Size L

MC ☐
CC ■

gusset placement ☐

Work Eye of Partridge patt on heel flap as foll:

Row 1: (WS) Sl 1 st wyf, [p1, sl 1 wyf] to last st, p1; turn work.

Row 2: (RS) Sl 1 wyb, k across; turn work.

Row 3: (WS) Sl 1 st wyf, [sl 1 wyf, p1] to last st, p1; turn work.

Row 4: (RS) Sl 1 wyb, k across; turn work.

Repeat Rows 1–4 until heel flap is 40 (42, 44) rows, ending after a WS Row. There will be 20 (21, 22) selvedge sts along each side of the heel flap.

TURN HEEL

Row 1: (RS) Sl 1 wyb, k16 (18, 20), ssk, k1; turn work.

Row 2: (WS) Sl 1 wyf, p7, p2tog, p1; turn work.

Row 3: Sl 1 wyb, k to 1 st before gap, ssk, k1; turn work.

Row 4: Sl 1 wyf, p to 1 st before gap, p2tog, p1; turn work.

Repeat Rows 3 and 4 until all sts have been worked—18 (20, 22) heel sts. Break MC.

GUSSET

Switch to larger needles. At the top corner of the heel flap, the CC is ready to be worked. Join MC and resume working in the rnd.

Next Rnd: M1 between the heel flap and the instep of the sock with MC (this is st 1 of Row 1 of the Funhouse chart), pick up and knit 15 (17, 19) sts along heel flap according to Row 1 of the Funhouse chart for your size (starting with st 2), pm to indicate start of gusset, pick up and knit 5 (4, 3) sts along heel flap according to Row 1 of the Gusset chart.

Cont Gusset chart along 18 (20, 22) heel flap sts, then pick up and knit the last 5 (4, 3) Gusset chart sts along the other side of the heel flap. Pm to indicate end of gusset. Pick up and knit 15 (17, 19) sts along heel flap according to Row 1 of the Funhouse chart (starting with st 17 [19, 21]). M1 between the heel flap and instep with MC (st 36 [38, 40] of the Funhouse chart for your size). Cont Row 1 across the instep—92 (100, 108) sts.

Gusset Rnd: Work Funhouse chart first half to first gusset m; work Gusset chart bet ms, work Funhouse chart to end. Cont in patt until Gusset chart has been completed.

Next Rnd: Work in patt to 1 st before first gusset m, sl 1, remove m, sl st from right needle back to left needle, ssk with MC (this corresponds to st 16 [18, 20] of chart), sl 1, remove m, sl st from right needle back to left needle, k2tog with MC (this corresponds to st 17 [19, 21] of chart); cont in patt to EOR—64 (72, 80) sts.

FOOT

Cont in patt until the foot measures about 1¼ (1½, 1¾)" (3 [4, 4.5] cm) less than the total desired length.

> *Note: Total length should be about ½" (1.5 cm) less than the foot that will wear it. Break CC yarn.*

TOE

Switch to smaller needles. Knit 1 rnd with MC.

Dec Rnd: [K6 (7, 8), k2tog] around—56 (64, 72) sts.

Gusset Chart

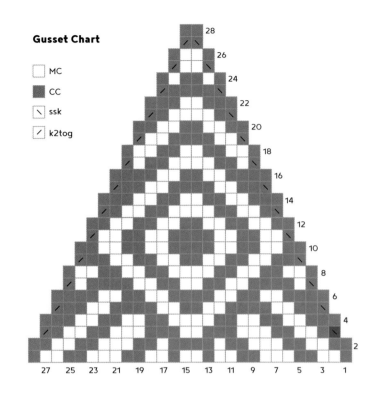

- ☐ MC
- ■ CC
- ╲ ssk
- ╱ k2tog

Rnd 1: Knit.

Rnd 2: K1, ssk, k to 3 sts before instep, k2tog, k1; k1, ssk, k to 3 sts before end of instep, k2tog, k1—4 sts dec'd.

Repeat Rnds 1 and 2 until 36 (40, 44) sts rem.

Repeat Rnd 2 until 20 (24, 24) sts rem.

finishing

Cut yarn, leaving a 12" (30 cm) tail. Divide sts evenly across two needles, and with tail threaded on a yarn needle, use Kitchener stitch (see Glossary) to graft toe closed.

To block, simply wash the socks. Weave in ends once dry.

ABOUT THE DESIGNER

Lisa K. Ross lives in Bloomington, Indiana, and is the mother of four boys. Her maiden name, "Stricker," means "knitter"—but she didn't pick up knitting until years after getting married. Since that time, she has rarely put down the needles, feeling that knitting is in her blood. Her obsession with sock knitting and fantasy has led her to create whimsical sock collections, such as the Socks of Wonderland and Socks of Wonka, which you can find on Ravelry.

meandros

— SANDI ROSNER —

THE GREEK KEY is a timeless classic. It can be found everywhere from ancient mosaic floors to contemporary bed linens and ceramics. Using a simple stripe for the heel, sole, and toe of these socks simplifies the shaping while providing a linear counterpoint to the meandering Greek key design. The intricate pattern on these socks is made entirely with slipped stitches, working with only one color in each round or row, and changing color every other row. This technique creates a fabric that's warm and sturdy, ideal for socks. Be sure to choose two colors with a distinct light/dark contrast to showcase the pattern. The sample shown uses hand-dyed near-solids, but this design would also be effective if one of the yarns were more highly variegated.

WORKED TOP DOWN, WITH A FLAP-AND-GUSSET HEEL & GRAFTED WEDGE TOE.

Finished Size
XS (S, M, L, XL)

Sock's foot circumference: 6½ (7, 7½, 8¼, 8¾)" (16.5 [18, 19, 21, 22] cm) to be worn with about ½" (1.5 cm) negative ease.

This fabric has less stretch than Stockinette, and for comfort, the socks need to be a little larger than for plain fabric.

Yarn
Fingering weight (#1 Super Fine).

Shown here: Hazel Knits Artisan Sock (90% superwash Merino, 10% nylon; 400 yds [366 m]/4¼ [120 g]): Viviane (MC), Tropical Sunset (CC), 1 skein each.

Needles
Size U.S. 2 (2.75 mm) needles: Your preferred configuration for small circumference in the round: DPNs, long circular for magic loop, 2 shorter circulars, set of three flexible DPNs, 8-9" (20-23 cm) circular.

Adjust needle size if necessary to obtain the correct gauge.

Notions
Stitch markers; stitch holder; yarn needle.

Gauge
38 sts and 54 rnds = 4" (10 cm) in Greek Key patt.

Notes
■ Unless directed otherwise, do not break the yarn when changing color. Carry the color not in use loosely along the inside of the sock until it's needed again.

■ All slipped stitches are worked as if to purl with the yarn held to the wrong side.

socks

Using the Old Norwegian Cast-On method (see Glossary), or the stretchy method of your choice, and MC, cast on 60 (66, 72, 78, 84) sts. Distribute sts across needles as you prefer and join for working in the rnd. Note or mark start of rnd as required.

CUFF

Rnd 1: [K2, p1] around.

Repeat Rnd 1 until cuff measures 1½" (4 cm).

LEG

With MC, knit 1 rnd.

Begin working Greek Key Chart. Work 20 rnds of patt 3 times, then work Rnds 1–10 once more. Piece measures about 6¾" (17 cm).

HEEL FLAP

Row 1: (RS) Work Row 1 of Stripe Chart over first 30 (36, 36, 42, 42) sts, turn work. Place remaining 30 (30, 36, 36, 42) sts on holder for instep.

Row 2: (WS) Work Row 2 of Stripe Chart.

Cont in Stripe Chart until a total of 30 (34, 38, 42, 46) rows have been worked on heel flap, ending with Row 2 of Stripe Chart. Break MC.

HEEL TURN

Row 1: (RS) With CC, [sl 1, k1] 8 (10, 10, 12, 12) times, sl 1, ssk, k1, turn.

Row 2: (WS) With CC, sl 1, p5 (7, 7, 9, 9), p2tog, p1, turn.

Row 3: With MC, [sl 1, k1] 3 (4, 4, 5, 5) times, sl 1, ssk, k1, turn.

Row 4: With MC, sl 1, p7 (9, 9, 11, 11), p2tog, p1, turn.

Row 5: With CC, [sl 1, k1] 4 (5, 5, 6, 6) times, sl 1, ssk, k1, turn.

Row 6: With CC, sl 1, p9 (11, 11, 13, 13), p2tog, p1, turn.

Row 7: With MC, [sl 1, k1] 5 (6, 6, 7, 7) times, sl 1, ssk, k1, turn.

Row 8: With MC, sl 1, p11 (13, 13, 15, 15), p2tog, p1, turn.

Row 9: With CC, [sl 1, k1] 6 (7, 7, 8, 8) times, sl 1, ssk, k1, turn.

Row 10: With CC, sl 1, p13 (15, 15, 17, 17), p2tog, p1, turn.

Row 11: With MC, [sl 1, k1] 7 (8, 8, 9, 9) times, sl 1, ssk, k1, turn.

Row 12: With MC, sl 1, p15 (17, 17, 19, 19), p2tog, p1, turn.

End of heel for size XS—18 sts remain on heel. Break CC.

Size S, M, L, XL Only
Row 13: With CC, [sl 1, k1] - (9, 9, 10, 10) times, sl 1, ssk, k1, turn.

Row 14: With CC, sl 1, p - (19, 19, 21, 21), p2tog, p1, turn.

End of heel for sizes S and M—22 sts remain on heel. Break CC.

Sizes L, XL Only
Row 15: With CC, [sl 1, k1] - (-, -, 11, 11) times, sl 1, ssk, k1, turn.

Row 16: With CC, sl 1, p - (-, -, 23, 23), p2tog, p1, turn.

End of heel for sizes X and XL—26 sts remain on heel. Break CC.

Greek Key Chart

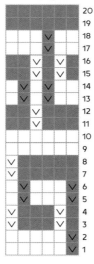

6-st patt rep

Stripe Chart

2-st patt rep

- ◼ MC: k on RS; p on WS
- ☐ CC: k on RS; p on WS
- ⊻ Sl1 with yarn on WS

GUSSET
All Sizes
Rnd 1: With MC, [sl 1, k1] 9 (11, 11, 13, 13) times, pick up and knit 14 (16, 16, 18, 18) sts along side of heel flap; this is the start of instep—pm or rearrange sts as you prefer; work Rnd 11 of Greek Key patt over 30 (30, 36, 36, 42) instep sts from holder; this is the new start of rnd—pm or rearrange sts as you prefer; pick up and knit 14 (16, 16, 18, 18) sts along other side of heel flap. Break MC. Slip 14 (16, 16, 18, 18) sts from right-hand needle to left-hand needle and rejoin MC at new BOR—76 (84, 90, 98, 104) sts.

Rnd 2: With MC, knit to start of instep, work Rnd 12 of Greek Key patt to end.

Rnd 3: With CC, k1, ssk, sl 1, [k1, sl 1] to 4 sts before start of instep, k1, k2tog, k1, work next rnd of Greek Key patt to end—2 sts dec'd.

Rnd 4: With CC, knit to m, work next rnd of Greek Key patt to end.

Rnd 5: With MC, k1, ssk, [sl 1, k1] to 3 sts before m, k2tog, k1, sl m, work next rnd of Greek Key patt to end—2 sts dec'd.

Rnd 6: With MC, knit to m, work next rnd of Greek Key patt to end.

Repeat Rnds 3–6 [3 (3, 3, 4, 4)] more times, then work Rnds 3 and 4 [0 (1, 1, 0, 0)] more times—60 (66, 72, 78, 84) sts.

FOOT

Maintaining patterns as set, work Stripe patt to m, sl m, work Greek Key patt to end. Work even until foot measures 1¾ (1¾, 2, 2, 2¼)" (4.5 [4.5, 5, 5, 5.5] cm) less than desired finished length (if you don't know the length of the foot you're knitting for, the sock should be approximately 7 (7¾, 8½, 9¼, 10)" (18 [19.5, 21.5, 23.5, 25.5] cm) at this point), ending with Rnd 10 or 20 of Greek Key patt.

TOE

Note: Depending on the size you're making and how long you worked for the foot, you could be starting the toe with either Rnd 1 or Rnd 3 of the Stripe patt. Maintain continuity of Stripe patt throughout the toe shaping. Decreases are worked on the plain knit rnds of patt.

Sizes S, L Only

Setup Rnd: Work next rnd of Stripe patt to EOR.

Next Rnd: K2, ssk, k - (28, -, 34, -), k2tog, knit to end— - (64, -, 76, -) sts.

All Sizes

Rnd 1: Work next rnd of Stripe patt to EOR.

Rnd 2: K2, ssk, knit to 4 sts before instep, k2tog, k2, ssk, knit to last 2 sts, k2tog—4 sts dec'd.

Repeat Rnds 1 and 2 [11 (12, 13, 14, 16)] more times—12 (12, 16, 16, 16) sts remain.

Knit first st of next rnd. Break both colors, leaving a tail 18" (45 cm) long of the color used to work the final row.

finishing

Divide sts evenly across two needles, and with tail threaded on a yarn needle, use Kitchener stitch (see Glossary) to graft toe closed.

To block, simply wash the socks. Weave in ends once dry.

ABOUT THE DESIGNER

Sandi Rosner has made her living as a knitter for almost twenty years. She has been a yarn shop owner, designer, technical editor, teacher, writer, and yarn company creative director. She's the author of four books, most recently, 21 Crocheted Tanks + Tunics: Stylish Designs for Every Occasion *(Stackpole Books). Sandi is a California native who now lives in Charlotte, North Carolina.*

— MONE DRÄGER —

mesmerizing

THESE COZY, WARM socks feature an interesting stitch pattern called "Mesmerized," drawn from Andrea Rangel's book, *AlterKnit Stitch Dictionary: 200 Modern Knitting Motifs*. Other than the cuff and the toe, which are worked only in the main color, the rest of the work is stranded knitting. The most eye-catching feature is their hybrid fleegle heel, which is worked in the round and emerges from the zigzagging stripes.

WORKED TOP DOWN, WITH AN INTEGRATED-GUSSET HEEL & A GRAFTED WEDGE TOE.

Finished Size
S (M, L)

Sock's foot circumference: 7 (8, 9)" (18 [20.5, 23] cm) to be worn with about ½" (1.5 cm) positive ease.

Yarn
Fingering weight (#1 Super Fine).

Shown here: Ancient Arts Yarn Socknado (80% superwash Merino, 20% nylon; 385 yds [353 m]/3½ oz [100 g]): Le Chat Noir (MC), Flamboyant (CC), 1 hank each.

Needles
Size U.S. 1½ (2.5 mm): Your preferred configuration for small circumference in the round: DPNs, long circular for magic loop, 2 shorter circulars, set of three flexible DPNs, 8-9" (20-23 cm) circular.

Size U.S. 2 (2.75 mm): Your preferred configuration for small circumference in the round: DPNs, long circular for magic loop, 2 shorter circulars, set of three flexible DPNs, 8-9" (20-23 cm) circular.

Adjust needle size if necessary to obtain the correct gauge.

Notions
Stitch markers; yarn needle.

Gauge
32 sts and 44 rnds = 4" (10 cm) in Stockinette st on smaller needles.

32 sts and 38 rnds = 4" (10 cm) in stranded knitting on larger needles.

Notes
■ The socks are worked in the round from the cuff down. The heel flap and gusset are worked as a so-called hybrid fleegle heel and are worked in the round, integrated into the leg pattern. The increases are made within the zigzagging stripes as follows: work 1 stitch in the appropriate color, make 1 stitch in the same color, work 1 (2) stitch(es) in the same color. Other than that, as these stripes get wider there is no change to the overall pattern.

■ The integrated heel section needs to be worked in full to achieve the correct stitch count, and the patterning relies on you ending the leg pattern on the round indicated. To adjust the leg length, start the leg chart in a different position: either before the stated round number to add length or after the stated round number to subtract length.

socks

With smaller needles and MC, CO 56 (64, 72) sts. Distribute sts across needles as you prefer and join for working in the round. Note or mark start of round as required.

CUFF

Ribbing Rnd: [K2, p2] around.

Work ribbing as set for 16 rnds total.

RIGHT SOCK

LEG

Switch to larger needles. Join CC.

Leg Rnd: Work Leg Chart around, starting with Rnd 11 (6, 1)—work the 4-st repeat to the last 4 sts of the rnd, then work the last 4 sts of the chart.

> **Note:** *This might seem to break patt, but the last 4 sts are set up specifically to reduce the look of the jog, and to make the transition to the heel seamless.*

Work as set until you have completed Rnd 20, then work Rnds 1–20, and cont until you have completed 12 (8, 4) rnds of the next repeat.

INTEGRATED HEEL

Work from Right Heel Chart for your size until Rnds 1–28 (1–32, 1–36) have been completed—84 (96, 108) sts. Break yarn.

TURN HEEL

Note: The heel will be turned over all stripes with 4 stitches.

Setup Row: Sl 33 (37, 41) sts. The heel turn will be worked over the 24 (28, 32) sts just slipped and the next 32 (36, 40) sts; total of 56 (64, 72) sts for the heel. Keep rem 28 (32, 36) sts on hold for instep.

Rejoin both yarns at this point.

Row 1: (RS) [With MC k1, with CC k1] 3 times, with MC k1, with CC ssk, k1, turn.

Row 2: (WS) Sl 1 wyf, [with CC p1, with MC p1] 3 times, with CC p1, with MC p2tog, p1, turn.

Row 3: Sl 1 wyb, [with CC k1, with MC k1] to 1 st before the gap, with CC ssk, k1, turn.

Row 4: Sl 1 wyf, [with CC p1, with MC p1] to 2 sts before the gap, with CC p1, with MC p2tog, p1, turn.

Repeat Rows 3 and 4 [8 (10, 12)] more times.

Row 5: Sl 1 wyb, [with CC k1, with MC k1] to 1 st before the gap, with CC ssk, turn.

Row 6: Sl 1 wyf, [with MC p1, with CC p1] to 1 st before the gap, with MC p2tog, turn.

Row 7: Sl 1 wyb, [with MC k1, with CC k1] to 1 st before the gap, with MC ssk, turn.

Row 8: Sl 1 wyf, [with CC p1, with MC p1] to 1 st before the gap, with CC p2tog, turn.

Repeat Rows 5-7 one more time. Do not turn after last row—29 (33, 37) sole sts; 57 (65, 73) sts total.

Leg Chart

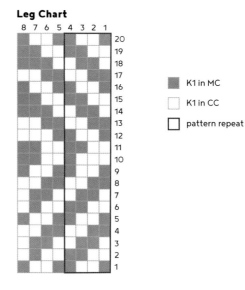

K1 in MC
K1 in CC
pattern repeat

Left Instep Chart   **Right Instep Chart**

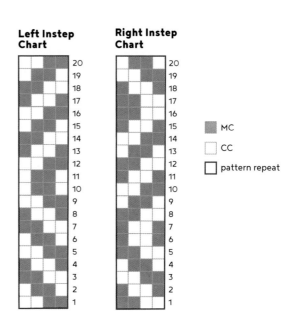

MC
CC
pattern repeat

Right Heel Chart, Size S

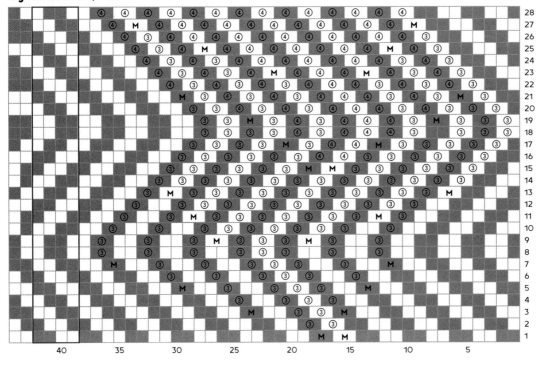

Right Heel Chart, Size M

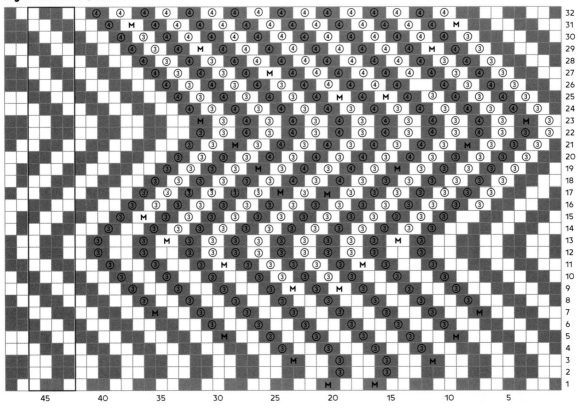

Right Heel Chart, Size L

Left Heel Chart, Size S

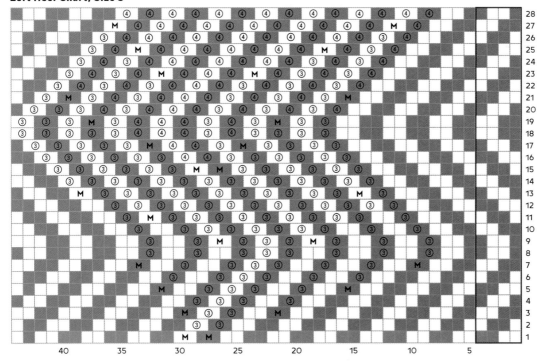

K1 in MC

K1 in CC

M M1* in MC

M M1* in CC

③ K3 in MC

③ K3 in CC

④ K4 in MC

④ K4 in CC

pattern repeat

*For M1, work 1 stitch in
appropriate color, make 1
stitch in the same color,
work 1 (2) stitch(es) in
the same color.*

Left Heel Chart, Size M

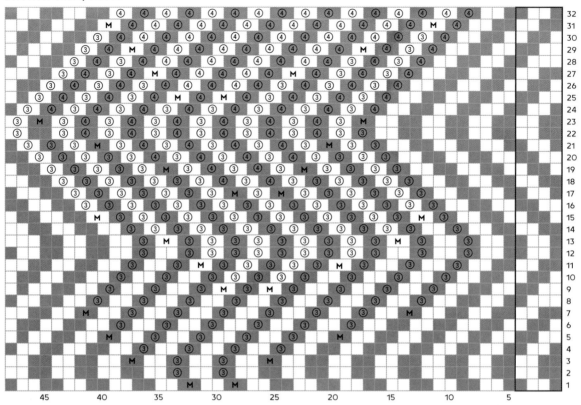

Left Heel Chart, Size L

FOOT

Note: Resume working in the rnd. This is the new BOR; place marker or rearrange sts as you prefer.

Setup Rnd: Work across 28 (32, 36) instep sts as per Right Instep Chart; with CC k2tog, [with MC k1, with CC k1] to last st, with MC k1—56 (64, 72) sts.

Rnds 1–2: Work across instep in patt as set, [with MC k1, with CC k1] to end.

Rnds 3–4: Work across instep in patt as set, [with CC k1, with MC k1] to end.

Cont in patt as set, working charted patt on instep and patt as set in Rnds 1–4 on sole, until foot measures 1¾ (2¼, 2½)" (4.5 [5.5, 6.5] cm) less than the desired length. Break CC.

TOE

Switch to smaller needles. Knit 3 rnds.

Dec Rnd: *K1, ssk, k to 3 sts before end of instep, k2tog, k2; ssk, k to 3 sts before EOR, k2tog, k1—4 sts dec'd.

Knit 2 rnds.

Repeat last 3 rnds once more—48 (56, 64) sts.

Work Dec Rnd, then knit 1 rnd.

Repeat last 2 rnds 2 (4, 6) more times—36 sts.

Work Dec Rnd 5 more times—16 sts.

LEFT SOCK

CUFF
Work as for Right Sock.

LEG
Switch to larger needles. Join CC.

Leg Rnd: Work Leg Chart around, starting with Rnd 1 (16, 11)—work the 4-st repeat to the last 4 sts of the rnd, then work the last 4 sts of the chart.

Note: This might seem to break patt, but the last 4 sts are set up specifically to reduce the look of the jog, and to make the transition to the heel seamless.

Work as set until you have completed Rnd 20, then work Rnds 1–20, and cont until you have completed Rnd 1 (17, 13) of the next repeat.

Next Rnd: Work Rnd 2 (18, 14) to last st, stopping at this point.

INTEGRATED HEEL
Work as for Right Sock, using Left Heel Chart for your size in place of Right Heel Chart.

TURN HEEL
Setup Rnd: Sl 43 (51, 59) sts. The heel turn will be worked over the 24 (28, 32) sts just slipped and the next 32 (36, 40) sts; total of 56 (64, 72) sts for the heel. Keep remaining 28 (32, 36) sts on hold for instep. Cont as for Right Sock.

FOOT & TOE
Work as for Right Sock, using Left Instep Chart.

finishing

Cut yarn, leaving a 12" (30 cm) tail. Divide sts evenly across two needles, and with tail threaded on a yarn needle, use Kitchener stitch (see Glossary) to graft toe closed.

To block, simply wash the socks and stretch on sock blockers.

▪	K1 in MC
□	K1 in CC
M	M1* in MC
M	M1* in CC
③	K3 in MC
③	K3 in CC
④	K4 in MC
④	K4 in CC
□	pattern repeat

* For M1, work 1 stitch in appropriate color, make 1 stitch in the same color, work 1 (2) stitch(es) in the same color.

ABOUT THE DESIGNER

Mone Dräger lives in a village in Germany. She loves to craft and be creative and can't imagine a day without knitting. She plays with colors and stitch patterns as she knits accessories and her favorite necessity—socks. Find her on social media as @monemade.

TWISTED STITCHES wave alongside a column of beautifully cabled stitches in a sweet little sashay, hence the affectionate name for these socks. They were inspired by a love of lithography, wood prints, and hammered metals—anything that gives surface dimension and has strong lines and texture. Beginning with a Turkish CO, you'll make a long gusset to a Strong heel. The socks are shaped from the ankle to allow for a lovely fit around the calf.

WORKED TOE-UP WITH AN INTEGRATED-GUSSET STRONG HEEL.

Finished Size

XS (S, M, L, XL)

Sock's foot circumference: 7 (7½, 8, 8½, 9)" (18 [19, 20.5, 21.5, 23] cm) to be worn with about 1" (2.5 cm) of negative ease.

Yarn

Fingering weight (#1 Super Fine).

Shown here: Knitted Wit Sock (80% superwash Merino, 20% nylon; 420 yd [384 m]/ 4 oz [113 g]): Tupelo Honey, 1 skein.

Needles

Size U.S. 2½ (3 mm): Your preferred configuration for small circumference in the round: DPNs, long circular for magic loop, 2 shorter circulars, set of three flexible DPNs, 8-9" (20-23 cm) circular.

Adjust needle size if necessary to obtain the correct gauge.

Notions

Stitch markers; cable needle; yarn needle.

Gauge

28 sts and 44 rnds = 4" (10 cm) in Stockinette st.

STITCH GUIDE

1/3 LC: Slip 1 st to cable needle and hold in front of work; k3; k1 from cable needle.

1/3 RC: Slip 3 sts to cable needle and hold in back of work; k1; k3 from cable needle.

1/1 RPT: Slip 1 st to cable needle and hold in back of work; k1 tbl; p1 from cable needle.

1/1 LPT: Slip 1 st to cable needle and hold in front of work; p1; k1 tbl from cable needle.

1/1 RC: Slip 1 st to cable needle and hold in back of work; k1; k1 from cable needle.

1/1 LC: Slip 1 st to cable needle and hold in front of work; k1; k1 from cable needle.

sashay

— MOIRA ENGEL —

socks
TOE

Using the Turkish Cast-On method (see Glossary), CO 12 (12, 14, 14, 16) sts—for a total of 24 (24, 28, 28, 32) stitches.

The first half of the stitches form the instep, the second half form the sole. Distribute sts or place markers as required.

Rnd 1: K1, M1L, knit to 1 st before end of instep m, M1R, k2, M1L, knit to 1 st before EOR, M1R, k1—4 sts inc'd.

Rnd 2: Knit.

Repeat Rnds 1 and 2 until you have 48 (52, 56, 60, 64) sts.

FOOT

> *Note: Use the Tuts Chart for your size—sizes XS and S are both in one chart, and sizes M, L, and XL are combined in another.*

Next Rnd: K0 (1, 0, 1, 2), work chart for your size, k0 (1, 0, 1, 2), k to end.

Work patt as set until foot measures 3½ (3½, 4, 4½, 4½)" (9 [9, 10, 11.5, 11.5] cm) short of desired finished foot length.

GUSSET

Rnd 1: Work in patt as set to sole, k1, M1L, knit to 1 st before end m, M1R, k1—2 sts inc'd.

Rnd 2: Work even in patt as set.

Repeat Rnds 1 and 2 [5 (5, 5, 6, 6)] more times—60 (64, 68, 74, 78) sts total.

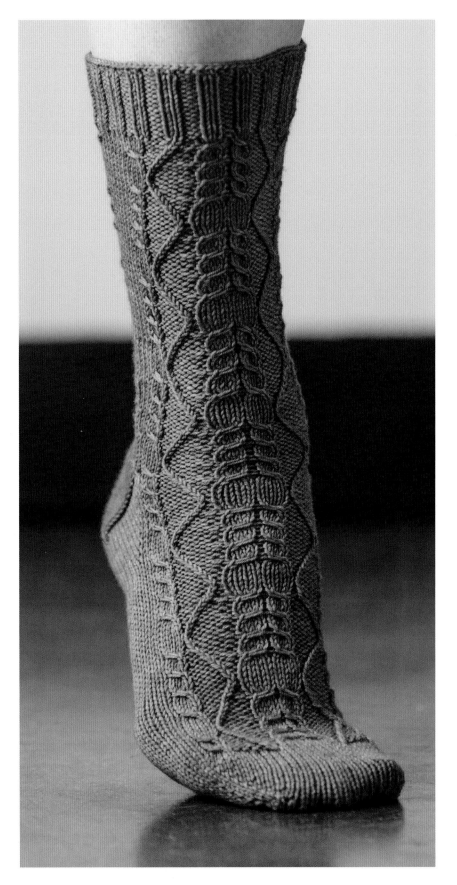

Tuts Chart, Sizes XS and S

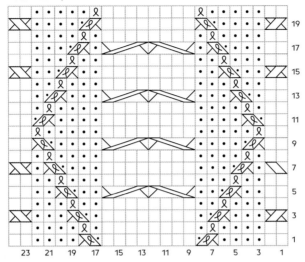

23 21 19 17 15 13 11 9 7 5 3 1

Tuts Chart, Sizes M, L, and XL

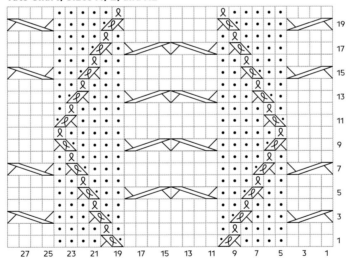

27 25 23 21 19 17 15 13 11 9 7 5 3 1

☐ knit	▱ 1/1 RC*	▱ 1/3 LC*
• purl	▱ 1/1 LC*	▱ 1/3 RC*
⏀ k1tbl	▱ 1/1 RPT*	*see stitch guide*
	▱ 1/1 LPT*	

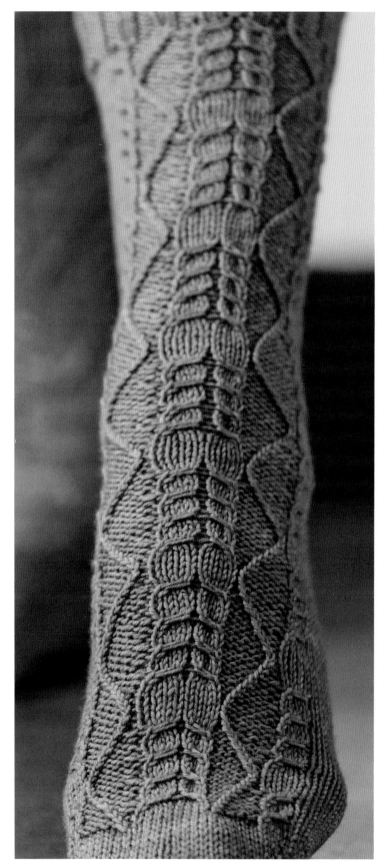

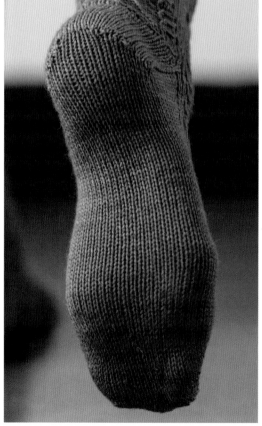

HEEL TURN

Rnd 1: Work 49 (52, 56, 60, 64) sts in patt, making note of last chart rnd worked. Turn.

The heel turn will be worked over the 14 (14, 16, 16, 18) sts just worked—group them together on one needle.

Row 1: (WS) P2tog, purl to end of heel sts, turn—1 st dec'd.

Row 2: Ssk, k to end of heel sts, turn—1 st dec'd.

Repeat Rows 1 and 2 until 4 (4, 6, 6, 8) heel sts remain.

HEEL FLAP

Next Rnd: Pick up and knit 10 sts along dec edge, k next 11 (12, 12, 14, 14) sts to end of rnd.

Next Row, Setup for Gusset Dec: Work patt as set across top of foot, k11 (12, 12, 14, 14) sts to gap; pick up and knit 10 sts along 2nd dec edge. K2 (2, 3, 3, 4) to center of heel—70 (74, 78, 84, 88) sts.

Row 1: K11 (12, 13, 14, 15), ssk. Turn.

Row 2: Sl 1 wyf, p22 (24, 26, 28, 30), p2tog; turn—1 st dec'd.

Row 3: Sl 1 wyb, k22 (24, 26, 28, 30), ssk; turn—1 st dec'd.

Row 4: Sl 1 wyf, p22 (24, 26, 28, 30), p2tog; turn—1 st dec'd.

Repeat Rows 3 and 4 [9 (9, 9, 10, 10)] more times—48 (52, 56, 60, 64) sts rem.

Next Row: K to EOR.

LEG

At this point you will resume working in the rnd; start working chart across sole/back of leg sts, picking up at the same place you are in the instep sts.

Leg Rnd: [K0 (1, 0, 1, 2), work chart for your size, k0 (1, 0, 1, 2)] twice.

Work in patt for 1" (2.5 cm).

Inc Rnd: Work in patt as set across instep, k0 (1, 0, 1, 2), M1L, work in patt to last 0 (1, 0, 1, 2) sts, M1R, k to end—2 sts inc'd.

Repeat Inc Rnd every 6th rnd 3 more times—56 (60, 64, 68, 72) sts. Cont even in patt until piece measures 9 (9½, 9¾, 10, 10¼)" (23 [24, 25, 25.5, 26] cm) from the base of the heel.

CUFF

Ribbing Rnd: [K2, p2] around.

Work ribbing as set for 1½" (3.8 cm).

Final Rnd: [Work 3 sts in rib, k1f&b] around.

BO as follows: *K2tog tbl; sl resulting st back to left needle; rep from * until all sts have been worked. Cut yarn and pull through final st to secure.

finishing

To block, simply wash the socks. Weave in ends once dry.

— AUD BERGO —

funambulus

THESE SLIPPER SOCKS take full advantage of cabling, yielding footwear with lots of texture and creating a flexible and stretchy fabric that forms nicely around your tootsies. If you're new to knitting cables, it might seem complex, but only until you've mastered the technique. Then comes the great reward, pleasure, and pride in having the technique under control.

WORKED TOP DOWN, WITH A FLAP-AND-GUSSET HEEL & CINCHED WEDGE TOE.

Finished Size

XS (S, M, L, XL)

Sock's foot circumference: 7½ (8, 8½, 9, 9½)" (19 [20.5, 21.5, 23, 24] cm).

Choose a size with approximately 1" (2.5 cm) negative ease in the foot circumference.

Yarn

Fingering weight (#1 Super Fine).

Shown here: Purl SOHO Posy (75% superwash Merino, 15% cashmere, 10% nylon; 318 yd [290 m]/3½ oz [100 g]): #3160P Pink Papaya, 1 (1, 2, 2, 2) skein.

Needles

Size U.S. 1½ (2.5 mm): Your preferred configuration for small circumference in the round: DPNs, long circular for magic loop, 2 shorter circulars, set of three flexible DPNs, 8–9" (20–23 cm) circular.

Adjust needle size if necessary to obtain the correct gauge.

Notions

Two cable needles; yarn needle.

Gauge

29 sts and 44 rnds = 4" (10 cm) in Stockinette st.

41 sts and 40 rnds = 4" (10 cm) in Leg stitch patt.

STITCH GUIDE

YOP2SO (Rib with Yarn Over Loop), 2 sts: Yo, knit 2 sts, pass the yo lp over the 2 knit sts.

FC6 (Fancy Cable), 6 sts: Slip 2 sts to cable needle and hold in back of work, slip the next 2 sts onto second cable needle and hold in front of work; k2; k2 from second cable needle; k2 from first cable needle.

2/2 RC: Slip 2 sts to cable needle and hold in back of work; k2; k2 from cable needle.

2/2 LC: Slip 2 sts to cable needle and hold in front of work; k2; k2 from cable needle.

socks

CO 64 (68, 72, 76, 82) sts. Turn work and k all sts. Distribute sts across needles as you prefer and join for working in the rnd. Note or mark start of rnd as required. The first 32 (34, 36, 40, 40) sts form the back of leg/heel/sole; the rem 32 (34, 36, 36, 42) sts form the front of leg/instep. Purl 1 rnd.

CUFF & LEG

Leg Rnd: Work Chart A Leg for appropriate size across 32 (34, 36, 40, 40) back of leg sts and Chart B Leg for appropriate size to EOR.

Work as set until you have completed 63 (67, 67, 67, 67) rnds—48 rows of Chart B, and 15 (19, 19, 19, 19) rnds of Chart A repeat ending with Row 3.

Setup for heel: Work next rnd of Chart A across back of leg sts and stop here.

HEEL FLAP

Turn work so that WS is facing.

Heel Flap Row 1: (WS) Work Chart C Heel Flap in the appropriate size across 32 (34, 36, 40, 40) sts.

Work as set until Heel Flap measures 2½–2¾" (6.5–7 cm), ending with a RS row.

Chart A, Sizes XS, S, L, and XL—Leg Back

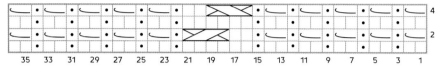

Chart A, Size M—Leg Back

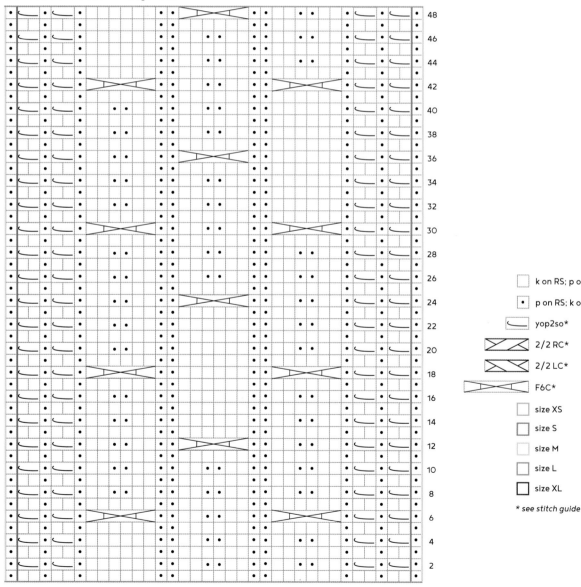

Chart B, Sizes S and M—Leg Front

□ k on RS; p on WS

• p on RS; k on WS

⌣ yop2so*

⬓ 2/2 RC*

⬓ 2/2 LC*

▭ F6C*

□ size XS

□ size S

□ size M

□ size L

□ size XL

see stitch guide

Chart B, Sizes XS, L, and XL—Leg Front

Legend:

- ☐ k on RS; p on WS
- ☐ • p on RS; k on WS
- ‿ yop2so*
- 2/2 RC*
- 2/2 LC*
- F6C*

- ☐ size XS
- ☐ size L
- ☐ size XL

* see stitch guide

Chart C, Size XS—Heel Flap

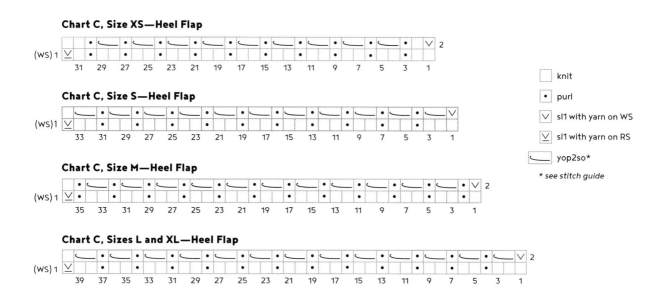

(WS) 1 ... 2
31 29 27 25 23 21 19 17 15 13 11 9 7 5 3 1

Chart C, Size S—Heel Flap

(WS) 1
33 31 29 27 25 23 21 19 17 15 13 11 9 7 5 3 1

Chart C, Size M—Heel Flap

(WS) 1 ... 2
35 33 31 29 27 25 23 21 19 17 15 13 11 9 7 5 3 1

Chart C, Sizes L and XL—Heel Flap

(WS) 1 ... 2
39 37 35 33 31 29 27 25 23 21 19 17 15 13 11 9 7 5 3 1

	knit
•	purl
⌄	sl1 with yarn on WS
⌄	sl1 with yarn on RS
⌣	yop2so*

see stitch guide

TURN HEEL

Row 1: (WS) Sl 1 wyf, p18 (18, 20, 22, 22), p2tog, p1, turn.

Row 2: (RS) Sl 1 wyb, k7 (5, 7, 7, 7), ssk, k1, turn.

Row 3: Sl 1 wyf, p to 1 st before gap, p2tog, p1, turn.

Row 4: Sl 1 wyb, k to 1 st before gap, ssk, k1, turn.

Repeat Rows 3 and 4 until all sts have been worked—20 (20, 22, 24, 24) sts rem. Cut yarn.

Chart D, Size XS—Gusset and Sole

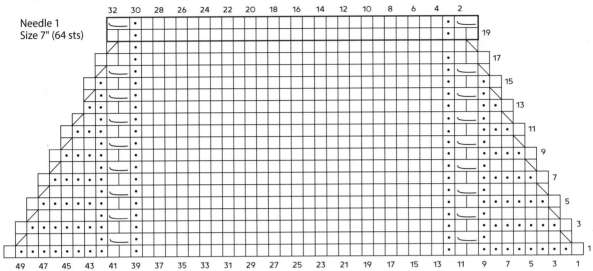

Needle 1
Size 7" (64 sts)

Chart D, Size S—Gusset and Sole

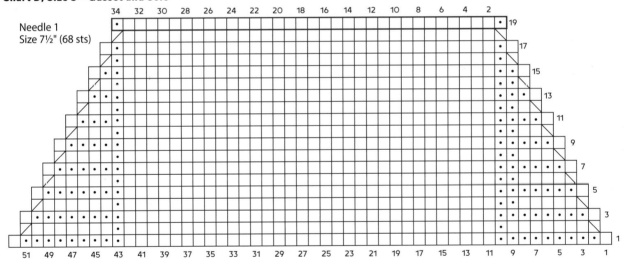

Needle 1
Size 7½" (68 sts)

Chart D, Size M—Gusset and Sole

Needle 1
Size 8" (72 sts)

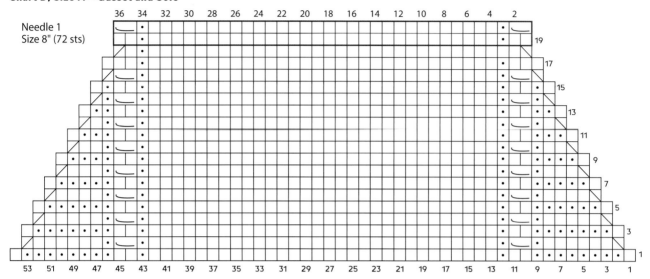

Chart D, Size L—Gusset and Sole

Needle 1
Size 8½" (76 sts)

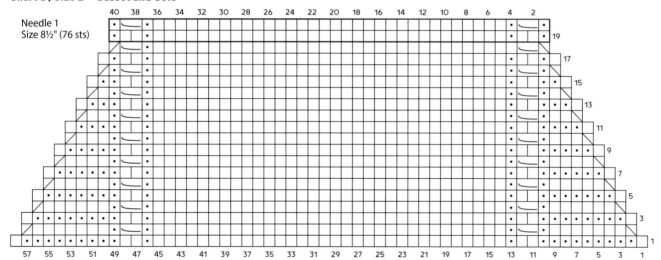

- ☐ knit
- • purl
- ⌣ yop2so*

see stitch guide

Chart D, Size XL—Gusset and Sole

Needle 1
Size XL
Size 9" (82 sts)

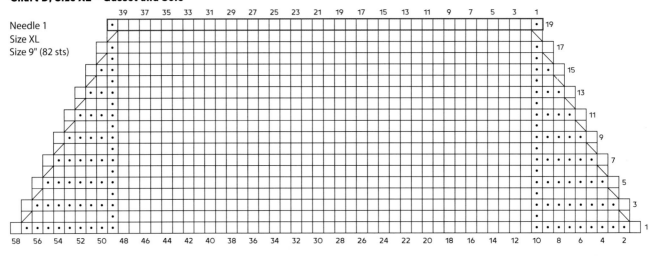

k on RS; p on WS

• p on RS; k on WS

GUSSET

Rejoin yarn at the end of the instep. With RS facing, starting at this position, pick up and knit 15 (16, 16, 17, 17) sts evenly spaced across the right side of the heel flap; knit across rem heel sts, and then pick up and knit 15 (16, 16, 17, 17) sts on the left side of the heel flap—82 (86, 90, 94, 100) sts.

Distribute sts across needles as you prefer and rejoin for working in the rnd. BOR is at the start of the instep.

Gusset Rnd: Work Chart B as set across instep; Work Chart D Gusset and Sole to EOR.

When gusset shaping is complete, 32 (34, 36, 40, 40) sts rem on the sole—64 (68, 72, 76, 82) sts total.

FOOT

Work even in patt as set until foot measures 1¼ (1½, 1½, 1½, 1¾, 1¾)" (3.2 [3.8, 3.8, 3.8, 4.5, 4.5] cm) short of desired finished length.

Size L Only

Move first sole sts to instep.

TOE

Rnd 1: Knit.

Rnd 2, dec: K1, ssk, k to last 3 sts of instep, k2tog, k2, ssk, k to last 3 sts of rnd, k2tog, k1—4 sts dec'd.

Repeat last 2 rnds 2 more times, then work Rnd 2 [10 (11, 12, 13, 14)] times—12 (12, 12, 12, 14) sts rem.

Cut yarn, leaving an 8" (20 cm) tail, thread tail through rem sts, pulling tight to close the hole, fasten off on WS.

finishing

To block, simply wash the socks. Weave in ends once dry.

downhill
both ways

— MEGAN WILLIAMS —

AS A PRECOCIOUS kid growing up a short, hilly bike ride away from the city pool, I always got a laugh when I mentioned to adults that my ride to the pool was "downhill both ways." I didn't understand that the saying "uphill both ways" implies quite the hardship, nor did I understand the pessimism; I instead reveled in the fun downhill portions where I zoomed along. These socks feature a fun biased construction and color play that will make knitting them feel like it's downhill both ways! The appealing pattern gives instructions for matching socks, mirrored socks, or inverted socks. It can be worked in a single color or in two contrasting colors. By working biasing wedges, biased texture sections, and then counterbalancing bias sections, you're in for an enjoyable knitting journey and striking socks to wear!

WORKED TOE-UP WITH A SHORT-ROW HEEL & MOCK GUSSET.

Finished Size
XS (S, M, L, XL)

Sock's foot circumference: 6 (7, 8, 9, 10)" (15 [18, 20.5, 23, 25.5] cm) to be worn with about ½" (1 cm) negative ease.

This fabric has less stretch than Stockinette, and for comfort, the socks need to be a little larger than for plain fabric.

Yarn
Fingering weight (#1 Super Fine).

Shown here: Leading Men Fiber Arts Show Stopper (75% superwash Merino, 25% nylon; 463 yd [423 m]/3½ oz [100 g]): Seaweed (MC), Metamorphosis (CC), 1 skein each.

Needles
Size U.S. 1 (2.25 mm): Your preferred configuration for small circumference in the round: DPNs, long circular for magic loop, 2 shorter circulars, set of three flexible DPNs, 8-9" (20-23 cm) circular.

Adjust needle size if necessary to obtain the correct gauge.

Notions
Stitch marker; yarn needle.

Gauge
32 sts and 48 rnds = 4" (10 cm) in Stockinette st.

socks
ROUNDED TOE

Using Judy's Magic Cast-On (see Glossary) and MC, CO 16 (16, 20, 20, 24) sts.

Setup Rnd: Knit.

Distribute sts or place markers so that you can identify the midpoint of the rnd.

Rnd 1: K1, M1L, k to last st of first half, M1R, k2, M1L, k to last st, M1R, k1—4 sts inc'd.

Rnd 2: K3, M1L, k to last 3 sts of first half, M1R, k6, M1L, k to last 3 sts, M1R, k3—4 sts inc'd.

Repeat Rnds 1 and 2 [0 (1, 1, 2, 2)] more times, and Rnd 1 [1 (0, 1, 0, 0)] more times—28 (32, 40, 44, 48) sts.

Rnd 3: Knit.

Rnd 4: Rep Rnd 1.

Repeat the last 2 rnds 4 (5, 5, 6, 7) more times—48 (56, 64, 72, 80) sts.

FOOT

Next Rnd: Knit.

Right Slant—Create Bias

Note: You're no longer working in the rnd; instead, you're working German short-rows (see Glossary) back and forth to create a wedge. Rows will cross the start of the rnd.

Short-row 1: (RS) K23 (27, 31, 35, 39), turn.

Short-row 2: (WS) DS, p46 (54, 62, 70, 78), turn.

Short-row 3: DS, k to 3 sts before the last DS (4 sts before the last turn gap), turn.

Short-row 4: DS, p to 3 sts before the last DS (4 sts before the last turn gap), turn.

Repeat Short-rows 3 and 4 until 5 sts remain between turn gaps, ending with a WS row. Resume working in the rnd.

When you come to a DS, work through both legs of DS.

Rnd 1: DS, k3 to BOR, working any DS through both legs.

Rnd 2: K all sts, working any DS through both legs to EOR.

Right Slant—Work Bias Motif

Join CC.

> **Note:** *The first half of the sts form the instep.*

Rnd 1: With CC, k1, M1L, k to last st of instep, M1R, k2, M1L, k to last st, M1R, k1—52 (60, 68, 76, 84) sts.

Rnd 2: With CC, p across first side; k to EOR.

Rnd 3: With MC, sl 1 wyb, [k3, sl 1] to 1 st before end of instep, k1; k to EOR.

Rnd 4: With CC, k1, [M1L, k2, k2tog] to last st of instep, k1; k1, ssk, k to last st, M1R, k1.

Repeat Rnds 3 and 4 eleven more times.

Rnd 5: With CC, p across instep; k to EOR.

Break CC, cont with MC.

Right Slant—Offset Bias

> **Note:** *You're no longer working in the rnd; you're working short-rows back and forth to create a wedge to balance the first wedge.*

Short-row 1: (RS) K27 (31, 35, 39, 43), turn.

Short-row 2: (WS) DS, p2, turn.

Short-row 3: DS, k to last DS, work DS through both legs, k4, turn.

Short-row 4: DS, p to last DS, work DS through both legs, p4, turn.

Repeat Short-rows 3 and 4 until you reach the EOR, ending with a WS row.

Resume working in the rnd.

Rnd 1: DS, k to EOR, working all DS through both legs.

Rnd 2: K around, working all DS through both legs.

Rnd 3, dec: K1, ssk, k to last 3 sts of instep, k2tog, k2, ssk, k to last 3 sts, k2tog, k1—48 (56, 64, 72, 80) sts.

Work even in St st with MC until foot measures ½ (1, 1, 1½, 1½)" (1.3 [2.5, 2.5, 3.8, 3.8] cm) less than desired total foot length.

Setup for heel: K to end of instep.

HEEL
MOCK GUSSET

Short-row 1: (RS) With MC, k1, M1R, [k2, M1R] 5 (6, 7, 8, 9) times, [k2, M1L] 6 (7, 8, 9, 10) times, k1—36 (42, 48, 54, 60) sts for heel. Rem sts are held.

Join CC, and work remainder of the heel with CC only.

Short-row 2: (WS) DS, p to end, turn.

Short-row 3: DS, k1, M1R, [k3, M1R] 5 (6, 7, 8, 9) times, k2, M1L, [k3, M1L] 5 (6, 7, 8, 9) times, k1; 1 st rem at end of heel, turn—12 (14, 16, 18, 20) sts inc'd; 48 (56, 64, 72, 80) sts; 12 (14, 16, 18, 20) gusset sts on each side.

TURN HEEL

Cont only on heel and gusset sts.

Short-row 4: DS, p to 1 st from the end, turn.

Short-row 5: DS, k to 12 (14, 16, 18, 20) sts from the end, turn.

Short-row 6: DS, p to 12 (14, 16, 18, 20) sts from the end, turn.

Short-row 7: DS, k to 1 st before last DS (2 sts before the last turn gap), turn.

Short-row 8: DS, p 1 st before last DS (2 sts before the last turn gap), turn.

Repeat Short-rows 7 and 8 [4 (5, 5, 6, 6)] more times, until 4 (4, 8, 8, 12) sts remain between turn gaps, ending with a WS row.

Short-row 9: (RS) DS, k to last 12 (14, 16, 18, 20) sts, working DS through both legs, turn.

Short-row 10: (WS) Sl 1 wyf, to last 12 (14, 16, 18, 20) sts, working DS through both legs, turn.

HEEL FLAP

Row 1: (RS) Sl 1 wyb, k22 (26, 30, 34, 38), ssk, turn—1 gusset st dec'd.

Row 2: (WS) Sl 1 wyf, [p1, sl 1] 11 (13, 15, 17, 19) times, p2tog, turn—1 gusset st dec'd.

Repeat Rows 1 and 2 [9 (11, 13, 15, 17)] more times until 2 sts remain on each gusset.

Repeat Rows 1 and 2 once more, noting that this gusset st is a DS, and you'll need to make sure you work both legs as one—1 gusset st rem on each side.

Last Row: (RS) Sl 1 wyb, k22 (26, 30, 34, 38), ssk. Do not turn.

Note: You'll work the remaining gusset DS on the other side of the heel flap together with the heel flap after working across the instep.

Break CC. Join MC and return to working in the rnd.

Next Rnd: K across instep; k2tog working both legs of gusset DS as one, k to EOR—48 (56, 64, 72, 80) sts.

LEG

First Leg Rnd: With MC, k around.

Left Slant—Create Bias

Note: Instead of working in the rnd, you're now working short-rows back and forth to create a wedge.

Short-row 1: (RS) K to last st, turn.

Short-row 2: (WS) DS, p to last st, turn.

Short-row 3: DS, k to 3 sts before the last DS (4 sts before the last turn gap), turn.

Short-row 4: DS, p to 3 sts before the last DS (4 sts before the last turn gap), turn.

Repeat Short-rows 3 and 4 until 5 sts remain between turn gaps, ending with a WS row. Resume working in the rnd.

Rnd 1: DS, k to end, working DS through both legs.

Rnd 2: K around, working DS through both legs.

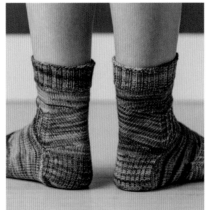

Left Slant—Work Bias Motif in the Rnd with MC and CC

Join CC.

Rnd 1: With CC, k1, M1L, k to last st of instep/front of leg, M1R, k2, M1L, k to last st, M1R, k1—52 (60, 68, 76, 84) sts.

Rnd 2: With CC, p across first side; k to EOR.

Rnd 3: With MC, sl 1 wyb, [k3, sl 1] to 1 st before end of instep, k1; k to EOR.

Rnd 4: With CC, k1, [SSK, k2, M1R] to last st of instep, k1; k1, ssk, k to last st, M1R, k1.

Repeat Rnds 3 and 4 eleven more times.

Last Rnd: P across instep, k to EOR.

Break CC, cont with MC.

Left Slant—Offset Bias

Note: You're no longer working in the rnd; you're working short-rows back and forth to create a wedge to unbias the sock. Rows will cross BOR.

Short-row 1: (RS) K1, turn.

Short-row 2: (WS) DS, p2, turn.

Short-row 3: DS, k to last DS, work both legs of DS, k4, turn.

Short-row 4: DS, p to last DS, work both legs of DS, p4, turn.

Repeat Short-rows 3 and 4 until 1 st rem between turn gaps, ending with a WS row. Resume working in the rnd.

Rnd 1: DS, k to end, working DS through both legs.

Rnd 2: K around, working DS through both legs.

Rnd 3, dec: K1, ssk, k to last 3 sts of instep/front of leg, k2tog, k2, ssk, k to last 3 sts k2tog, k1—48 (56, 64, 72, 80) sts.

Work even in St st with MC until leg measures 6 (6, 6½, 6½, 7)" (15 [15, 16.5, 16.5, 18] cm) long, or ½ (½, 1, 1½, 1½)" (1.3 [1.3, 2.5, 3.8, 3.8] cm) less than desired total leg length.

CUFF

Break MC, and join CC.

Next Rnd: Knit.

Next Rnd, ribbing: [K2, p2] around.

Work ribbing as set until cuff measures ½ (1, 1, 1½, 1½)" (1.5 [2.5, 2.5, 4, 4] cm).

BO in patt using your preferred stretchy BO.

SECOND SOCK

For matching socks: Work the 2nd sock the same as the first.

For mirrored socks: Work the Left Slant section on the foot, and the Right Slant section on the leg.

For inverted socks: Switch MC and CC and work either a mirrored or matching sock.

finishing

To block, simply wash the socks. Weave in ends once dry.

siddal

— CHERYL TOY —

ELIZABETH SIDDAL POSED extensively for the Pre-Raphaelite painters—in fact, you might call her the first supermodel. Named after her, these socks have bands of staggered lace patterning at the cuff that gradually ease into simple eyelet columns. Offset motifs continue into an eyelet-edged Strong heel. As the soles progress in Stockinette stitch, the motifs recur on the instep. The toes devolve into smooth Stockinette and are grafted using Kitchener stitch. Show off the patterning that continues into the heel by wearing these socks with sandals or clogs.

WORKED TOP-DOWN WITH AN INTEGRATED-GUSSET STRONG HEEL & GRAFTED WEDGE TOE.

Finished Size
XS (S, M, L, XL)

Sock's foot circumference: 7 (7¼, 7¾, 8¼, 8¾)" (18 [18.5, 19.5, 21, 22] cm) to be worn with about 1" (2.5 cm) negative ease.

Yarn
Fingering weight (#1 Super Fine).

Shown here: SweetGeorgia CashLuxe Fine (70% superwash Merino, 20% cashmere, 10% nylon; 400 yd [365 m]/4 oz [115 g]): Lollipop, 1 (1, 2, 2, 2) skein.

Needles
Size U.S. 1 (2.25 mm): Your preferred configuration for small circumference in the round: DPNs, long circular for magic loop, 2 shorter circulars, set of three flexible DPNs, 8-9" (20-23 cm) circular.

Adjust needle size if necessary to obtain the correct gauge.

Notions
Stitch markers; 1 removable marker; yarn needle.

Gauge
34 sts and 46 rnds = 4" (10 cm) in Stockinette st.

socks

Using the long-tail cast-on method (see Glossary), CO 72 (76, 80, 84, 88) sts. Distribute sts across needles as you prefer and join for working in the round. Note or mark start of round as required.

CUFF

Ribbing Rnd: [K1, p1] around.

Work ribbing as set until cuff measures 1" (2.5 cm).

LEG

Setup Rnd: [Work ribbing as set over next 5 (7, 9, 11, 13) sts, pm for start of chart (mA), work Chart A over next 31 sts, pm for end of chart] twice.

Cont as set until Rnd 10 of Chart A is complete.

Work Rnds 1–10 of Chart A once more, and then cont through to Rnd 22 of the chart.

AT THE SAME TIME work Dec Rnd as foll on Rnds 1 and 11 of chart.

Dec Rnd: [K2tog, knit to 2 sts before chart m, ssk, work Chart A across next 31 sts] twice—4 sts dec'd.

Cont until Rnd 10 is completed a second time, repeat Dec Rnd—64 (68, 72, 76, 80) sts.

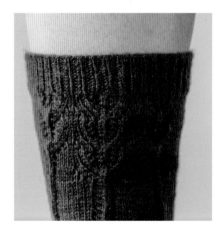

Chart A

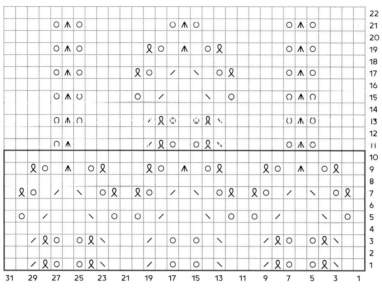

Legend:
- ☐ knit
- • purl
- O yo
- ℓ k1tbl
- ＼ ssk
- ／ k2tog
- ⋀ CDD*
- ☐ pattern repeat

see stitch guide

Size XS Only

Cont even, working through the end of Rnd 22 of Chart A.

Size S Only

Next Rnd: [CDD, work Chart A to next mA] twice—64 sts.

Sizes M, L, XL Only

Next Rnd: [K2tog, knit to 2 sts before mA, ssk, work Chart A] twice— - (-, 68, 72, 76) sts.

Sizes S, M, L, XL Only

Cont even until you have completed Rnd 22 of Chart A.

All Sizes

Cont even, repeating Rnds 21 and 22 of Chart A as set until sock measures 6 (6, 7, 7½, 8)" (15 [15, 18, 19, 20.5] cm) from CO edge, ending with Rnd 21.

Setup Rnd: K1 (1, 2, 3, 4); This is the new EOR; pm or rearrange sts as you prefer. K0 (0, 1, 2, 3) to chart m, work Rnd 22 of Chart A, k0 (0, 1, 2, 3); this is the midpoint of rnd, place markers or rearrange sts as you prefer, k1 (1, 2, 3, 4) to chart m, work Rnd 22 of Chart A, k1 (1, 2, 3, 4) to new EOR—first 31 (31, 33, 35, 37) sts are instep sts, next 33 (33, 35, 37, 39) sts are heel sts.

Next Rnd: K to chart m, work Rnd 21 of Chart A, knit to next chart m, work Rnd 1 of Chart B, knit to end.

Cont in St st repeating Rnds 21 and 22 of Chart A on instep until you have completed Rnd 10 of Chart B on heel sts.

GUSSET

Inc Rnd: Work in patt as set to midpoint of rnd, k1, yo, knit to chart m, work Chart B as set, knit to last st yo, k1—2 sts inc'd.

Next Rnd: Work even in patt as set.

Repeat the last 2 rnds [13 (15, 16, 17, 18)] more times, repeating Rnds 21 and 22 of Chart A on instep and working Chart B on heel sts until Chart B is complete. Once Chart B is complete, knit all heel sts—92 (96, 102, 108, 114) sts, 61 (65, 69, 73, 77) heel sts.

HEEL

Turn work to begin heel turn on a WS row.

Row 1: (WS) P33 (35, 37, 39, 41), p2tog, p1, turn.

Row 2: (RS) Sl 1 wyb, k6, ssk, k1, turn.

Row 3: Sl 1 wyf, purl to 1st before gap, p2tog across gap, p1, turn.

Row 4: Sl 1 wyb, knit to 1st before gap, ssk across gap, k1, turn.

Repeat Rows 3 and 4 [12 (13, 14, 15, 16)] more times—35 (37, 39, 41, 43) heel sts rem.

Next Row: (WS) Sl 1 wyf, purl to 1st before gap, p2tog across gap, turn.

Next Row: (RS) Sl 1 wyb, knit to 1st before gap, ssk across gap. Do not turn—33 (35, 37, 39, 41) heel sts rem.

FOOT

Place removable m directly in fabric on instep sts and resume working in the rnd.

Work 2 rnds even, keeping heel/sole sts in St st and working Rnds 21 and 22 of Chart A on instep as set.

Dec Rnd: Work across instep in patt as set, ssk, knit to last 2 sts of rnd, k2tog—2 sts dec'd.

Next Rnd: Work even in patt as set.

Repeat last 2 rnds once more—60 (62, 66, 70, 74) sts.

Cont even, repeating Rnds 21 and 22 of Chart A until foot measures 4¼" (11 cm) short of desired finished foot length.

Cont, working Chart B on the instep in place of Chart A, until all 30 rnds of Chart B are complete.

Chart B

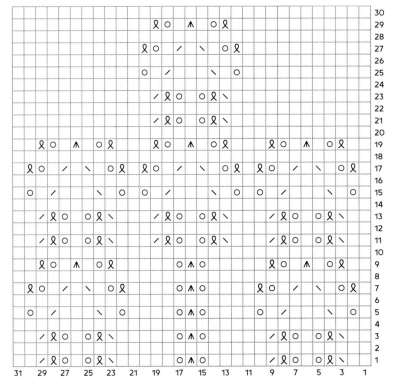

knit

• purl

O yo

Ꝗ k1tbl

\ ssk

/ k2tog

⋀ CDD*

see stitch guide

TOE

Size XS Only

Rearranging st or repositioning m as required, move the last st from the instep to the sole sts, shifting the midpoint of the rnd so that you have 30 sts on each side.

All Sizes

Dec Rnd: *K1, k2tog, knit to 3 sts before midpoint of rnd, ssk, k2, k2tog, k to 3 sts before EOR, ssk, k1—4 sts dec'd.

Next Rnd: Knit.

Repeat last 2 rnds 9 more times—20 (22, 26, 30, 34) sts.

finishing

Cut yarn, leaving a 12" (30 cm) tail. Divide sts evenly across two needles, and with tail threaded on a yarn needle, use Kitchener stitch (see Glossary) to graft toe closed.

To block, simply wash the socks. Weave in ends once dry.

ABOUT THE DESIGNER

From her tiny studio in New Orleans, Louisiana, Cheryl Toy avidly knits, teaches, and designs knitwear. A former set designer and art director for film and television, Cheryl frequently draws on historical references to create engaging knits that focus on simple, timeless shapes. Amusing details and quirky techniques fascinate her. Cheryl's work can be found in several books. She has contributed to Interweave Knits, Knitscene, and Knit.Wear magazines, and Brooklyn Tweed's Wool People 13.

i scream

— CAITLIN THOMSON —

I SCREAM, YOU scream, we all scream for ice cream socks! Everyone will want to wear this delicious knitted treat. Two-strand, colorwork charts help create the look of a melting ice cream cone on a warm summer day. With the option to change the length from ankle to mid calf by adding one, two, or three scoops of ice cream, the possibilities are endless. Depending on your scoop colors, you can make the socks any "flavor" you like. Use mini skeins for these "scoops," or stash bust. Pick contrasting colors to make the colorwork really stand out. The mock cable pattern worked on the foot uses slip stitches to create a waffle pattern that looks good enough to eat. Hurry up—cast on your sweet treat and watch your yarn stash melt away!

WORKED TOP DOWN, WITH A SHORT-ROW HEEL & GRAFTED WEDGE TOE.

Finished Size

XS (S, M, L, XL)

Sock's foot circumference: 5¼ (6¼, 7, 8, 9)" (13.5 [16, 18, 20.5, 23] cm) to be worn with about 1" (2.5 cm) negative ease.

Yarn

Fingering weight (#1 Super Fine).

Shown here: Wooly Wonka Rhiannon Sock (75% superwash Merino, 25% nylon; 465 yd [425 m]/3½ oz [100 g]): Waffle Cone (MC), 1 skein; (97 yd [89 m]/¾ oz [20 g]): Vanilla Sprinkles (CC1), Strawberry (CC2), Chocolate (CC3), 1 mini skein each.

Needles

Size U.S. 1½ (2.5 mm): Your preferred configuration for small circumference in the round: DPNs, long circular for magic loop, 2 shorter circulars, set of three flexible DPNs, 8–9" (20–23 cm) circular.

Adjust needle size if necessary to obtain the correct gauge.

Notions

Stitch marker; yarn needle.

Gauge

36 stitches and 40 rnds = 4" (10 cm) in Stockinette st.

36 stitches and 36 rnds = 4" (10 cm) in Waffle Cone st patt.

STITCH GUIDE

slLT (Slip Left Stitch): Work over two sts; slip first st and knit into the back of the second st. Leaving the second st on the needle, knit into the front of the skipped st. Slip both sts off together. This creates a raised st that leans to the left. When you reach this stitch, it should be knit like two stitches, although they can look very close together. This is not a decrease.

slRT (Slip Right Stitch): K2tog, leaving this resulting st on the left-hand needle, i.e., insert right-hand needle between sts just knitted together and knit the first st again; slip both sts to right needle.

SHWK (Shadow Wrap Knit): Lift the right leg of the st below the next one on the left needle, and place it up onto the left needle. Knit into it and slip the resulting st back to the left needle. This creates a "shadow" for the knit st.

SHWP (Shadow Wrap Purl): Slip the st you would like to shadow from the left to the right needle. Pick up the loop of the st below the working st, place it on the right-hand needle, and purl into it. Slip the purl and its shadow st back to the left needle.

socks

Using CC1 and the long-tail method, cast on 48 (56, 64, 72, 80) sts. Distribute sts across needles as you prefer and join for working in the round. Note or mark start of round as required.

CUFF

Next Rnd: [K1, p1] around.

Work ribbing as set until cuff measures about 1¼ (1¼, 1¼, 1½, 2)" (3 [3, 3, 4, 5] cm).

LEG

ICE CREAM SCOOPS

K for 1¼ (1¼, 1¼, 1½, 1¾)" (3 [3, 3, 4, 4.5] cm).

Next Rnd: Join CC2 and work Chart A as indicated for appropriate size around.

Once Chart A is complete, cut CC1 and knit with CC2 for about 1 (1, 1, 1¼, 1½)" (2.5 [2.5, 2.5, 3, 4] cm).

Next Rnd: Join CC3 and work Chart B as indicated for appropriate size around.

Once Chart B is complete, cut CC2 and knit with CC3 for about 1 (1, 1, 1¼, 1½)" (2.5 [2.5, 2.5, 3, 4] cm).

Chart A—Vanilla Scoop

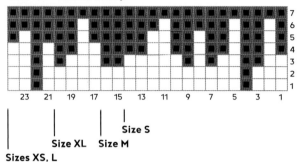

Sizes XS, L
Size XL   Size M
Size S

Chart B—Strawberry Scoop

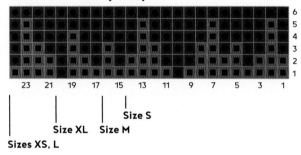

Sizes XS, L
Size XL   Size M
Size S

Chart C—Chocolate Scoop

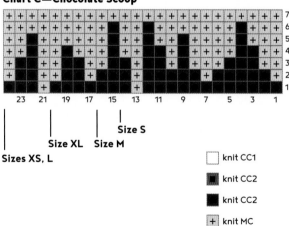

Sizes XS, L
Size XL   Size M
Size S

□ knit CC1
▣ knit CC2
■ knit CC2
⊞ knit MC

Next Rnd: Join MC and work Chart C as indicated for appropriate size around.

Cut CC3 and cont in MC.

WAFFLE CONE SETUP
All sizes

Rnd 1-3: Knit.

Rnd 4: Purl.

Rnd 5: Knit.

WAFFLE CONE
Rnd 1: [K6, sILT] around.

Rnd 2: K5, sIRT, sILT *[k4, sIRT, sILT] to last 7 sts, k4, sIRT, work sILT with the last st of the rnd and the first st of the next rnd, keeping the EOR in the middle of these two sts.

Rnd 3:
> *Note: The first st of the rnd has already been worked as part of the last twist.*

K3, [IRT, k2, sILT, k2] to last 4 stitches, sIRT, k2.

Rnd 4: K1, [sILT, sIRT, k4] to last 7 sts, sILT, sIRT, k3.

Rnd 5: K2, sILT, k6, [sILT, k6] to last 6 sts, sILT, k4.

Rnd 6: K1, sIRT, sILT, [k4, sIRT, sILT] to last 3 sts, k3.

Rnd 7: [SIRT, k2, sILT, k2] to last 7 sts, sIRT, k2, sILT, k1; work sIRT with the last st of the rnd and the first st of the next rnd, keeping the EOR in the middle of these two sts.

Rnd 8:
> *Note: The first st of the rnd has already been worked as part of the last twist.*

[K4, sILT, sIRT] to last 7 sts, k4, sILT, k1.

HEEL

Row 1: (RS) K9 (15, 17, 15, 25) SHWK, turn work—10 (16, 18, 16, 26) sts worked. These stitches plus the next 1 (unworked, unwrapped st) will become part of the heel: 11 (17, 19, 17, 27) sts total from the start of the round. Slip the following 24 (28, 32, 36, 40) sts to a holder or single needle—these will become the instep.

The heel turn is worked on 24 (28, 32, 36, 40) sts—11 (17, 19, 17, 27) sts from the start of the rnd (the sts worked, the SHWK st, and the following unworked st as noted above), and last 13 (11, 13, 19, 13) sts of the rnd. Rearrange sts as you prefer.

Row 2: (WS) P20 (24, 28, 32, 36) SHWP, turn work.

Row 3: (RS) K to 1 before SHWK, and work a SHWK, turn work.

Row 4: (WS) P to 1 stitch before SHWP, and work a SHWP, turn work.

Repeat Rows 3 and 4 until there are 7, (9, 10, 11, 13) SHW sts on each side of your heel, and 8 (8, 10, 12, 12) unwrapped stitches in the center. (The first and last of the heel sts are unwrapped.)

Next Row: (RS) K across all the SHWK sts, knitting the st and its shadow together as one, to the last st of the heel. SHWK, turn work.

Row 1: (WS) P across all the heel stitches purling the SHWP sts and their shadows together as one, to the last st of the heel. SHWP, turn work.

Row 2: (RS) K15 (17, 20, 23, 25) SHWK, turn work.

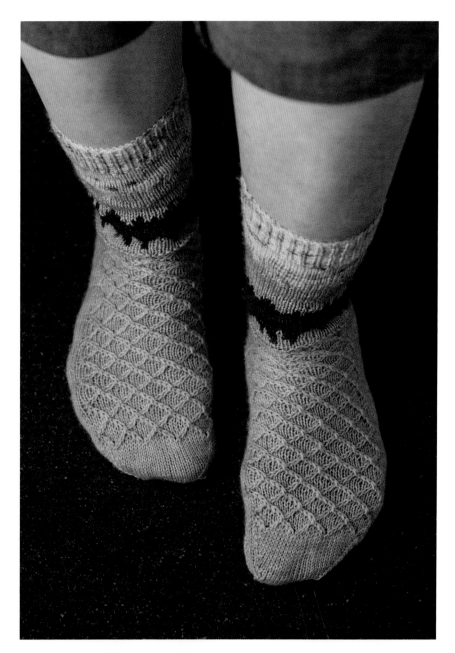

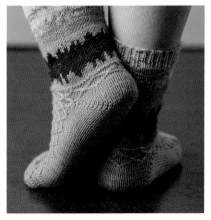

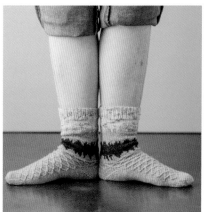

Row 3: P8 (8, 10, 12, 12) SHWP, turn work.

Row 4: K to SHWK, knit st and its shadow together as one, SHWK, turn work.

Row 5: P to SHWP, purl st and its shadow together as one, SHWP, turn work.

Repeat Rows 4 and 5 until you have worked all but one of the sts on either side. The heel should now have 2 SHWK and 2 SHWP on either side of heel stitches—the two stitches at either end.

Final Row: K to end of heel sts, knitting the 2 SHWK with their shadows.

FOOT
WAFFLE CONE
Sizes XS, M, L Only

Rnd 1: K3, sILT, [k6, sILT] to last 3 instep sts, k3; k to end of rnd, working those final two SHWK sts as you have been doing.

Rnd 2: [K2, sIRT, sILT, k2] across instep; k to end of rnd.

Rnd 3: [K1, sIRT, k2, sILT, k1] across instep; k to end of rnd.

Rnd 4: [SIRT, k4, sILT] across instep; k to end of rnd.

Rnd 5: K7, sILT, [k6, sILT] to last 7 instep sts, k7; k to end of rnd.

Rnd 6: [SILT, k4, sIRT] across instep; k to end of rnd.

Rnd 7: [K1, sILT, k2, sIRT, k1] across instep; k to end of rnd.

Rnd 8: [K2, sILT, sIRT, k2] across instep; k to end of rnd.

Repeat Rnds 1–8 until foot measures 1½ (–, 2¼, 2 ½, –)" (3.8 [–, 5.5, 6.5, –] cm) short of desired length.

Sizes S, XL Only

Rnd 1: K5, [sILT, k6] to last 7 instep sts, sILT, k5; k to end of rnd working those final two SHWK sts as you have been doing.

Rnd 2: [K4, sIRT, sILT] to last 4 instep sts, k4; k to end of rnd.

Rnd 3: K3, [sIRT, k2, sILT, k2] to last instep st, k1; k to end of rnd.

Rnd 4: K2, [sILT, k4, sILT] to last 2 sts, k2; k to end of rnd.

Rnd 5: K1, [sILT, k6] to last 3 instep sts, sILT, k1; k to end of rnd.

Rnd 6: K2, [sILT, k4, sIRT] to last 2 instep sts, k2; k to end of rnd.

Rnd 7: K3, [sILT, k2, sIRT, k2] to last instep st, k1; k to end of rnd.

Rnd 8: [K4, sILT, sIRT] to last 4 instep sts, k4; k to end of rnd.

Repeat Rnds 1–8 until foot measures – (1½, –, –, 2½)" (– [3.8, –, –, 6.5] cm) short of desired length.

TOE
All Sizes

Rnd 1: K to 3 sts before instep k2tog, k2, ssk; k to 3 sts before end of instep; k2tog, k2, ssk, k to EOR—4 sts dec'd.

Rnd 2: Knit.

Repeat Rnds 1 and 2 until 12 (16, 16, 20, 24) sts rem.

Setup for closure: K to start of instep.

finishing

Cut yarn, leaving a 12" (30 cm) tail. Divide sts evenly across two needles, and with tail threaded on a yarn needle, use Kitchener stitch (see Glossary) to graft toe closed.

To block, simply wash the socks. Weave in ends once dry.

THESE SOCKS FEATURE a simple cable pattern along the legs that continues onto the top of the foot. The pattern is mostly a 1 × 2 ribbing interrupted by mini cable twists that resemble little droplets of rain. With lots of space between cables, this pattern is perfect for knitters wanting a project with a little bit of detail that doesn't overwhelm with lots of cable work. The ribbed cables yield a stretchy fabric ideal for well-fitting socks. The leg is worked in the round, while the heel is worked flat and has an Eye of Partridge patterned heel flap. Stitches are picked up and the work is joined in the round again to work the Stockinette stitch gusset. The bottom of the foot is worked in Stockinette stitch while the cabled pattern continues on the top of the foot. The toe is a simple round toe finished with Kitchener stitch.

WORKED TOP DOWN, WITH A FLAP-AND-GUSSET HEEL & GRAFTED WEDGE TOE.

Finished Size
XS (S, M, L, XL)

Sock's foot circumference: 6 (7¼, 8½, 9¾, 11)" (15 [18.5, 21.5, 25, 28] cm) to be worn with about 1" (2.5 cm) negative ease.

Yarn
Fingering weight (#1 Super Fine).

Shown here: Malabrigo Sock (100% superwash Merino; 440 yds [402 m]/ 3½ oz [100 g]): #SW133 Reflecting Pool, 1 (1, 2, 2, 2) skein.

Needles
Size U.S. 1 (2.25 mm): Your preferred configuration for small circumference in the round: DPNs, long circular for magic loop, 2 shorter circulars, set of three flexible DPNs, 8-9" (20-23 cm) circular.

Adjust needle size if necessary to obtain the correct gauge.

Notions
Stitch markers; cable needle; yarn needle.

Gauge
36 sts and 52 rnds = 4" (10 cm) in Stockinette st.

STITCH GUIDE
1/1 RC: Slip 1 stitch to cable needle and hold in back of work; k1; k1 from cable needle.

1/1 RPC: Slip 1 stitch to cable needle and hold in back of work; k1; p1 from cable needle.

1/1 LPC: Slip 1 stitch to cable needle and hold in front of work; p1; k1 from cable needle.

gentle drizzle

— EMILY KINTIGH —

socks

Using your preferred stretchy method, CO 60 (72, 84, 96, 108) sts. Distribute sts across needles as you prefer and join for working in the round. Note or mark start of round as required.

CUFF

Ribbing Rnd: [P1, k1, p1] around.

Work ribbing as set for 16 rnds total.

LEG

Work from Gentle Drizzle Chart until sock measures 6½ (6¾, 7, 7¼, 7½)" (16.5 [17, 18, 18.5, 19] cm) from CO edge. Keep track of the last rnd of Gentle Drizzle Chart worked.

HEEL FLAP

Turn to work H Fl across 30 (36, 42, 48, 54) sts just worked.

Rows 1 and 3: (WS) K1, p28 (34, 40, 46, 52), sl 1 wyf.

Row 2: K1, [sl 1, k1] to last st, sl 1 wyf.

Row 4: K1, [k1, sl 1] to last st, sl 1 wyf.

Repeat Rows 1–4 [6 (8, 9, 11, 12)] more times, then Rows 1 and 2 [1 (0, 1, 0, 1)] more times—30 (36, 42, 48, 54) rows worked total.

HEEL TURN

Row 1: (WS) K1, p15 (18, 21, 24, 27), p2tog, p1, turn.

Row 2: Sl 1 wyb, k3, ssk, k1, turn.

Row 3: Sl 1 wyf, p to 1 st before gap, p2tog, p1, turn.

Row 4: Sl 1 wyb, k to 1 st before gap, ssk, k1, turn.

Repeat the last 2 rows 4 (6, 8, 10, 12) more times—18 (20, 24, 26, 30) sts rem.

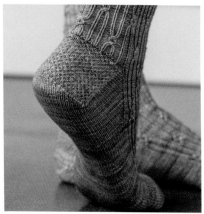

Sizes XS, M, XL Only

Next Row: Sl 1 wyf, p to 1 st before gap, p2tog, turn.

Final Row: Sl 1 wyb, k to 1 st before gap, ssk—16 (-, 22, -, 28) sts rem.

GUSSET

Gusset Setup Rnd: Pick up and knit 17 (20, 23, 26, 29) sts along side of heel flap, work across 30 (36, 42, 48, 54) instep sts continuing on the next rnd of the Gentle Drizzle Chart (working sts 1–12 of chart 2 [3, 3, 4, 4] times, then sts 1–6 of chart 1 [0, 1, 0, 1] time), pick up and knit 17 (20, 23, 26, 29) sts along side of heel flap, k8 (10, 11, 13, 14). This is the new EOR; pm or rearrange sts as you prefer—80 (96, 110, 126, 140) sts.

Rnd 1: K to 2 sts before end of instep, ssk, work Gentle Drizzle Chart as set across instep, k2tog, k to end—78 (94, 108, 124, 138) sts.

Rnd 2: K to 3 sts before instep, k2tog, k1, work Gentle Drizzle Chart as set across instep, k1, ssk, k to end—2 sts dec'd.

Rnd 3: Work even in patt as set.

Repeat Rnds 2 and 3 until 60 (72, 84, 96, 108) sts remain.

To set up for foot, k to start of instep. This is the new start of rnd; pm or rearrange sts as you prefer.

FOOT

Foot Rnd: Work Gentle Drizzle Chart as set over first 30 (36, 42, 48, 54) sts, k to EOR.

Repeat until foot measures approximately 1½ (1¾, 2, 2½, 2¾)" (4 [4.5, 5, 6.5, 7] cm) from desired length.

> *Note: It looks best if you end in the ribbed sections of the chart.*

TOE

Rnd 1: K to end.

Rnd 2: *Ssk, k to 2 sts before end of instep, k2tog; ssk, k to last 2 sts, k2tog—4 sts dec'd.

Repeat Rnds 1 and 2 [6 (8, 9, 11, 12)] more times—32 (36, 44, 48, 56) sts rem.

Work Rnd 2 [4 (4, 5, 6, 7)] times—16 (20, 24, 24, 28) sts remain.

finishing

Cut yarn, leaving a 12" (30 cm) tail. Divide sts evenly across two needles, and with tail threaded on a yarn needle, use Kitchener stitch (see Glossary) to graft toe closed.

To block, simply wash the socks. Weave in ends once dry.

Gentle Drizzle Chart

☐ knit	◪ 1/1 RPC*
• purl	◪ 1/1 LPC*
◪ 1/1 RC*	* see stitch guide

ABOUT THE DESIGNER

Emily Kintigh works as an educational assistant in Eugene, Oregon, which allows her to design knitting patterns in her off time. Find other things she has designed—toys, accessories, and more—on Ravelry under her name.

better half

— NATALIYA SINELSHCHIKOVA —

WHEN WORN WITH the feet side by side, the symmetrically laid-out triangles on the toes of these socks form the shape of a heart. This pattern was created to celebrate affection and care, making the socks the perfect gift for a loved one. Intarsia, twisted stitches, and lace elements will keep you engaged with the knitting. So, if you're looking for a pattern to learn some new techniques or enhance your skills, Better Half might be right up your alley. To highlight the beautiful relief created by twisted stitches, use solid or semisolid colors. Play around with bright color combinations to create festive moods and brighten up a dull day, or choose pastel shades for a more romantic tone.

WORKED TOE-UP WITH A SHORT-ROW HEEL.

Finished Size

XS (S, M, L, XL)

Sock's foot circumference. 6¾ (7¼, 7¾, 8½, 9)" (17 [18.5, 19.5, 21.5, 23] cm) to be worn with about ½-1" (1.5-2.5 cm) negative ease.

Yarn

Fingering weight (#1 Super Fine).

Shown here: Miss Babs Hot Shot (80% superwash Merino, 20% nylon; 400 yd [365 m]/4 oz [115 g]): Quicksilver (MC), Ruby Spinel (CC), 1 skein each.

Needles

Size U.S. 1 (2.25 mm): Your preferred configuration for small circumference in the round: DPNs, long circular for magic loop, 2 shorter circulars, set of three flexible DPNs, 8-9" (20-23 cm) circular.

Adjust needle size if necessary to obtain the correct gauge.

Notions

Stitch markers; stitch holder or scrap yarn; yarn needle.

Gauge

28 sts and 38 rnds = 4" (10 cm) in Stockinette st.

Notes

■ Instructions are to be worked for both socks unless separate instructions are specified for Right Sock and Left Sock.

■ Patterning is worked with Intarsia technique. To work Intarsia in the rnd, odd rnds should be worked on the right side and even rnds on the wrong side using the Invisible Join method. This method uses yarnovers and decreases worked on alternate RS and WS rows to keep the piece joined.

■ Twist yarn threads when switching colors to avoid holes.

STITCH GUIDE

RT2 (Right Twist): K2tog leaving sts on left-hand needle, then k the first st again, slipping sts off needle.

LT2 (Left Twist): Skip next st, k following st through back loop leaving st on left-hand needle, k skipped st through front loop, slipping both sts off needle.

socks
TOE (FOR BOTH SOCKS)

Using Judy's Magic Cast-On (see Glossary) and CC, CO 16 (16, 20, 20, 20) sts.

Rnd 1: Knit around, dividing sts at the midpoint of the round for the instep and the sole; pm or rearrange sts as you prefer.

Rnd 2: [K1, LLI, knit to 1 st before midpoint of rnd, RLI, k2] twice—4 sts inc'd.

Repeat Rnd 2 [2 (2, 2, 3, 3)] more times—28 (28, 32, 36, 36) sts.

Rnd 3: Knit.

Rnd 4: Repeat Rnd 2.

Repeat Rnds 3 and 4 [4 (4, 5, 5, 6)] more times—48 (52, 56, 60, 64) sts.

Rnd 5: Knit.

FOOT

Turn piece to work from WS.

> **Note:** M indicates end of rnds. You will place and remove the marker after each row, to help you keep track of the rnds. Rm after completing each rnd.

LEFT SOCK

Setup Rnd 1: (RS) Join new strand of MC, sk next st, with MC knit foll st on left-hand needle through back loop leaving st on left-hand needle, change from MC to CC (do not add new strand), with CC k sk st through front loop, slipping both sts off needle, with CC LT2 11 (12, 13, 14, 15) times, k to 1 st before EOR, join new strand of MC, with MC k1, turn work.

Setup Rnd 2: (WS) With MC yo, pm, p1, change to CC, with CC p to 2 st before m, change to MC, with MC p2tog, rm, turn work.

Cont by following Left Chart starting from Row 17 (13, 9, 5, 1). Work the first and last 2 columns of the chart, and then the sts indicated for your size.

RIGHT SOCK

Setup Rnd 1: (RS) Join new strand of MC, with MC k1, change from MC to CC (do not add new strand), k23 (25, 27, 29, 31), RT2 11 (12, 13, 14, 15) times, with CC k2tog leaving sts on left-hand needle, join new strand of MC, change from CC to MC, with MC k the first st again, slipping sts off needle, rm, turn work.

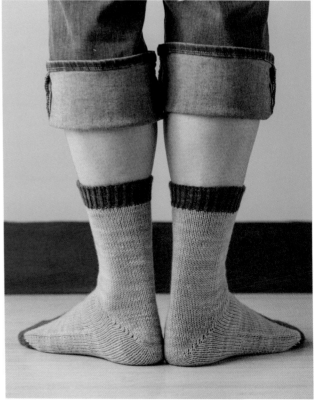

Left Chart

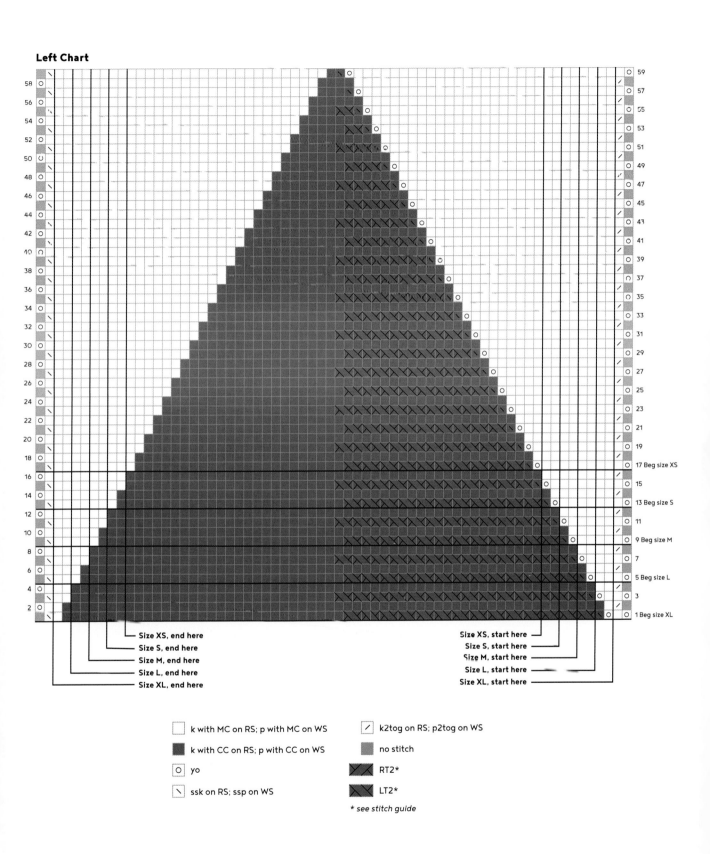

Size XS, end here
Size S, end here
Size M, end here
Size L, end here
Size XL, end here

Size XS, start here
Size S, start here
Size M, start here
Size L, start here
Size XL, start here

	k with MC on RS; p with MC on WS		✓	k2tog on RS; p2tog on WS
	k with CC on RS; p with CC on WS			no stitch
O	yo			RT2*
\	ssk on RS; ssp on WS			LT2*

see stitch guide

Right Chart

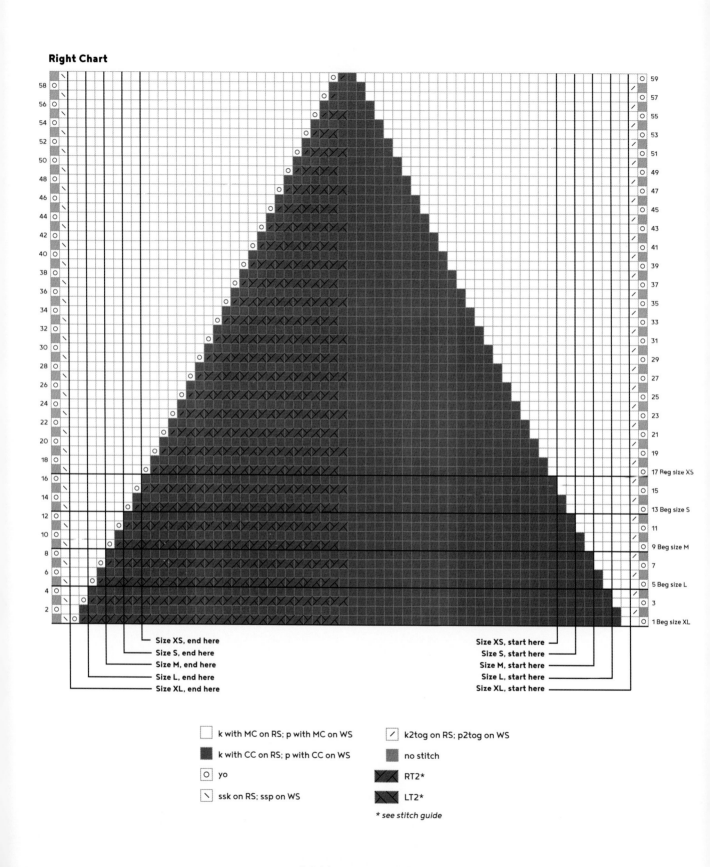

Size XS, end here
Size S, end here
Size M, end here
Size L, end here
Size XL, end here

Size XS, start here
Size S, start here
Size M, start here
Size L, start here
Size XL, start here

☐ k with MC on RS; p with MC on WS	⟋ k2tog on RS; p2tog on WS
◼ k with CC on RS; p with CC on WS	◼ no stitch
O yo	◼ RT2*
⟍ ssk on RS; ssp on WS	◼ LT2*
	see stitch guide

Setup Rnd 2: (WS) With MC yo, pm, p1, change to CC, with CC p to 2 st before m, change to MC, with MC p2tog, rm, turn work.

Cont by following Right Chart starting from Row 17 (13, 9, 5, 1). Work the first and last 2 columns of the chart, and then the sts indicated for your size.

Note: Both socks are worked the same way from Foot through Finishing.

FOOT

After chart is completed, do not turn work. Cut CC, and cont working in the rnd with MC. Work in Stockinette st patt until foot measures approx 1.75 (2, 2, 2.25, 2.5)" (4.5 [5, 5, 5.5, 6] cm) less than desired foot length.

HEEL

K24 (26, 28, 30, 32). These sts will be held for instep; slip them onto a stitch holder or group them together on one needle as desired.

Work across the rem 24 (26, 28, 30, 32) sts for the heel as foll:

PART 1
All Sizes
Short-row 1: (RS) K24 (26, 28, 30, 32), turn.

Short-row 2: (WS) DS (see Abbreviations), p23 (25, 27, 29, 31), turn.

Short-row 3: DS, k to previous DS, turn.

Short-row 4: DS, p to previous DS, turn.

Repeat Short-rows 3 and 4 [6 (7, 7, 8, 9)] more times, ending with a WS row.

PART 2
Note: As you come to each DS work through both legs.

Short-row 1: (RS) DS, k to previous DS, [work DS through both legs] twice, turn.

Short-row 2: (WS) DS, P to previous DS, [work DS through both legs] twice, turn.

Repeat Short-rows 1 and 2 [5 (6, 6, 7, 8)] more times, and work Short-row 1 once more. WS is facing.

Next row: (WS) Sl 1 wyf, p23 (25, 27, 29, 31), turn.

Next row: Sl 1 wyb, k23 (25, 27, 29, 31).

LEG

Work in St st in the rnd until leg measures approx 1½" (4 cm) less than the desired leg length.

Note: To avoid little holes pick up a stitch between the sole and instep stitches in the first leg rnd by lifting the bar between the needles and knitting it together with the next stitch.

CUFF

Break MC. Join CC.

Rnd 1: With CC, k.

Rnds 2–14: [K1 tbl, p1] around.

BO all stitches using Jeny's Surprisingly Stretchy Bind-Off (see Glossary) or preferred stretchy method.

finishing

To block, simply wash the socks. Weave in ends once dry.

ABOUT THE DESIGNER

Nataliya Sinelshchikova is a graphic designer and media artist by day and a passionate knitter and crafter the rest of the time. Born in Moscow, Russia, she moved to The Netherlands in 2015, where she began knitting. In 2017 her first-ever pattern, Pink Pine Pair, was published in Amirisu. Nataliya focuses on modern wearable items with a twist. Her pattern recipe: smart design, good fit, eye-catching details, and captivating colors—shaken, not stirred! Ravelry: FibreCreative. Instagram: @fibre_creative.

THESE ELEGANT SOCKS are enveloped in a delicate, cabled heart design, framed with tight twists, and offset by an Eye of Partridge slip-stitch heel for style and durability. The tiled cabled pattern starts off exciting and seemingly chaotic, but quickly settles down into comforting predictability as the cables entwine themselves around each other in a texture far simpler to knit than it looks. Whether you're dancing on air with new love, walking hand-in-hand with an old love, or still on the arduous journey of finding love, these are the socks for your feet because Love Needs a Heart.

WORKED TOE-UP WITH A GUSSET & FLAP HEEL.

Finished Size
XS (S, M, L, XL)

Sock's foot circumference: 6 (7, 8, 9, 9½)" (15 [18, 20.5, 23, 24] cm) to be worn with about 1" (2.5 cm) negative ease.

Yarn
Light fingering weight (#0 Lace).

Shown here: Coop Knits Socks Yeah! (75% Merino, 25% nylon; 231 yd [212 m]/1¾ oz [50 g]): #104 Sphene, 2 (2, 2, 3, 3) skeins.

Needles
Size U.S. 1 (2.25 mm): Your preferred configuration for small circumference in the round: DPNs, long circular for magic loop, 2 shorter circulars, set of three flexible DPNs, 8-9" (20-23 cm) circular.

Adjust needle size if necessary to obtain the correct gauge.

Notions
Stitch markers; cable needle; yarn needle.

Gauge
40 sts and 48 rnds = 4" (10 cm) in Stockinette st.

Notes
■ Working the knit st below 1/2 LPC and 1/2 RPC sts slightly looser will form smoother outlines to the hearts.

STITCH GUIDE
1/1 RC: Slip 1 stitch to cable needle and hold in back of work; k1; k1 from cable needle.

1/1 RPC: Slip 1 stitch to cable needle and hold in back of work; k1; p1 from cable needle.

1/1 LC: Slip 1 stitch to cable needle and hold in front of work; k1; k1 from cable needle.

1/1 LPC: Slip 1 stitch to cable needle and hold in front of work; p1; k1 from cable needle.

1/2 LPC: Slip 1 stitch to cable needle and hold in front of work; p2; k1 from cable needle.

1/2 RPC: Slip 2 stitches to cable needle and hold in back of work; k1; p2 from cable needle.

love needs a heart

— NICOLE WAGENBLAST —

socks
TOE

Using Judy's Magic Cast-On method (see Glossary), CO 28 (32, 36, 40, 36) sts.

Rnd 1: Knitting through the back loop as required to avoid twisted sts, knit around. The first half of the sts form the instep; the second half form the sole. Pm or rearrange sts as you prefer.

Rnd 2: K1, M1R, k to last st of instep, M1L, k2, M1R, k to last st, M1L, k1—4 sts inc'd.

Rnd 3: K.

Repeat Rnds 2 and 3 [1 (1, 2, 4, 2)] more times.

Repeat Rnd 2 one more time— 40 (44, 52, 64, 52) sts total.

Next Rnd: Work appropriate size Toe and Instep Chart across instep sts, k1, M1R, k to last st, M1L, k1—4 sts inc'd.

Next Rnd: Work appropriate size Toe and Instep Chart as set, k to end of rnd.

Repeat the last 2 rnds until Rnd 10 (12, 4, 2, 20) of chart is complete—30 (34, 30, 34, 46) sts on instep, 30 (34, 30, 34, 46) sts on sole.

Next Rnd: Work appropriate size Toe and Instep Chart across instep sts, k to end of rnd.

Work as set until Rnd 29 (29, 40, 44, 40) of chart is complete—34 (38, 50, 56, 50) sts on instep; 30 (34, 30, 34, 46) sts on sole; 64 (72, 80, 90, 96) sts total.

Once toe increases are complete, repeat Rows 22-41 (22-41, 32-51, 32-51, 32-51) of the Toe and Instep Chart.

FOOT

Foot Rnd: Work instep in patt (repeating Rows 22-41 [22-41, 32-51, 32-51, 32-51] as noted above) for your size; k to EOR.

Work patt as set until foot measures 3¼ (3½, 3¾, 3¾, 4)" (8.5 [9, 9.5, 9.5, 10] cm) short of desired foot length.

GUSSET

Rnd 1, inc: Work instep in patt as set; M1L, pm, k to EOR, pm, M1R—2 sts inc'd.

Rnd 2: Work instep in patt as set; k to end of rnd.

Rnd 3, inc: Work instep in patt as set, k to next m, M1L, sm, k to next m, sm, M1R, k to EOR—2 sts inc'd.

Repeat Rnds 2 and 3 [9 (10, 12, 13, 14)] more times; 11 (12, 14, 15, 16) gusset sts between the markers on each side of the bottom sts—86 (96, 108, 120, 128) sts total.

Make a note of the last instep patt row worked.

Toe and Instep Chart, Size S

Toe and Instep Chart, Size XS

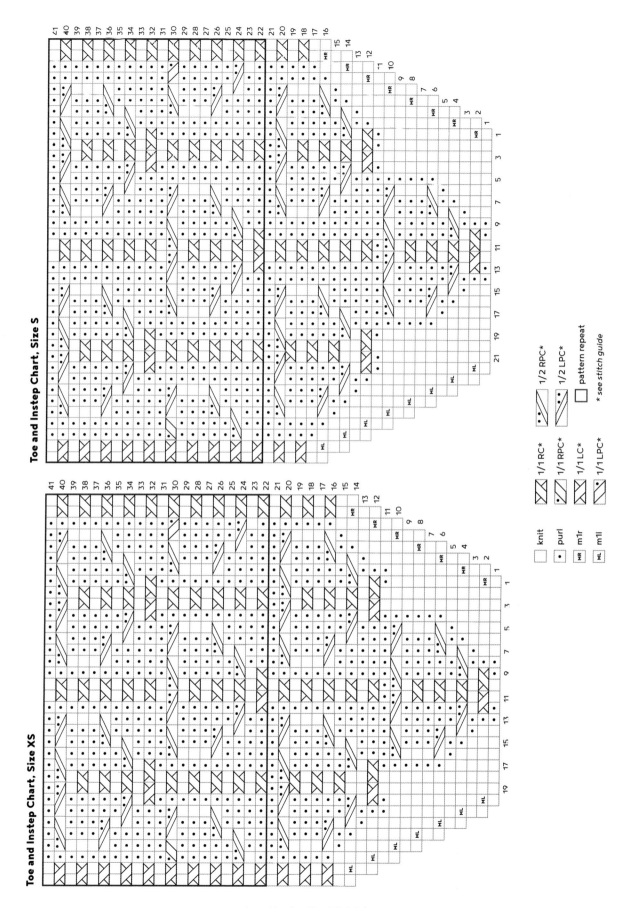

	knit		1/1 RC*		1/2 RPC*
•	purl		1/1 RPC*		1/2 LPC*
MR	m1r		1/1 LC*		pattern repeat
ML	m1l		1/1 LPC*		* see stitch guide

Toe and Instep Chart, Sizes M and XL

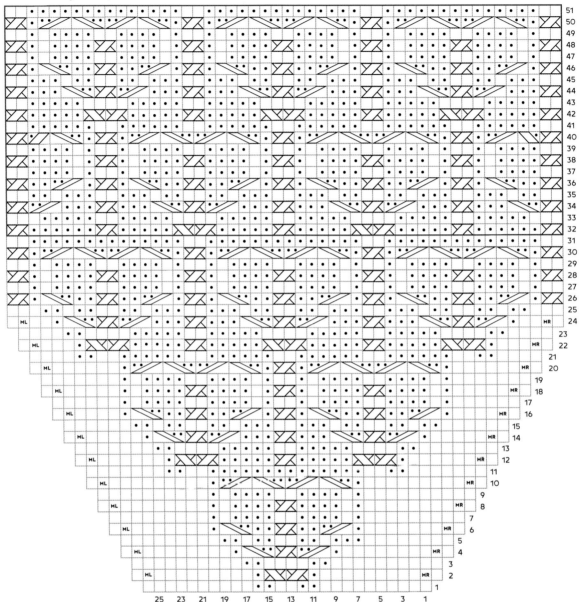

Toe and Instep Chart, Size L

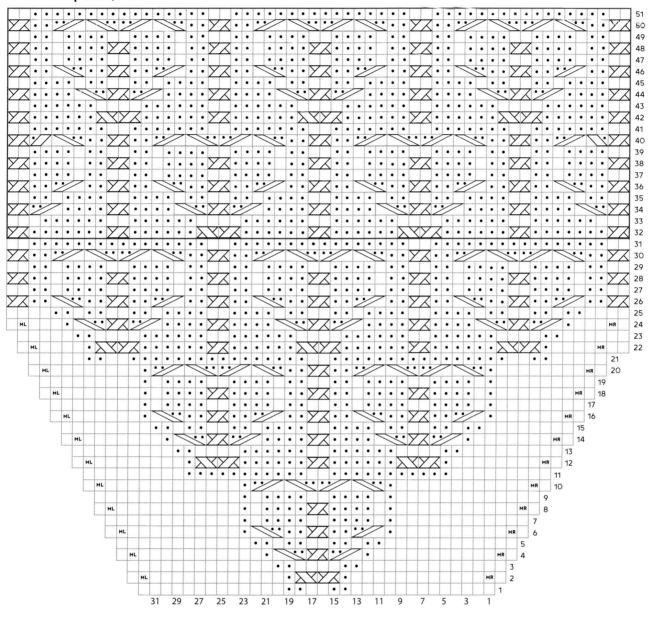

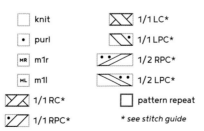

	knit		1/1 LC*
	purl		1/1 LPC*
ML	m1r		1/2 RPC*
ML	m1l		1/2 LPC*
	1/1 RC*		pattern repeat
	1/1 RPC*		*see stitch guide*

HEEL TURN

Short-row 1: (RS) Work instep sts in patt, k11 (12, 14, 15, 16) gusset sts, k29 (33, 29, 33, 45) sts, w&t (see Glossary).

Short-row 2: (WS) P28 (32, 28, 32, 44) sts, w&t.

Short-row 3: K to 1 st before the last wrapped st, w&t.

Short-row 4: P to 1 st before the last wrapped st, w&t.

Repeat Short-rows 3 and 4 until 10 (12, 10, 12, 15) sts rem unwrapped in the center, with 10 (11, 10, 11, 16) wrapped sts on each side.

Next Row: (RS) K10 (12, 10, 12, 15) unwrapped stitches, k9 (10, 9, 10, 14) wrapped sts together with their wraps, 1 wrapped st rem; work ssk on the final wrapped st, its wrap and the first of the gusset sts, removing m indicating the edge of the gusset stitches.

Next Row: (WS) Sl 1 wyf, p19 (22, 19, 22, 29), p9 (10, 9, 10, 14) wrapped sts together with their wraps. P the last heel stitch, together with its wrap and the first gusset stitch as p2tog, rm indicating the edge of the gusset stitches, turn.

Next Row: Sl 1 purlwise wyb, k28 (32, 28, 32, 44), ssk, turn.

HEEL FLAP

Row 1: (WS) Sl 1 purlwise wyf, p28 (32, 28, 32, 44), ssp, turn.

Row 2: (RS) Sl 1 purlwise wyb, [k1, sl 1] 14 (16, 14, 16, 22) times, ssk, turn.

Row 3: Rep Row 1.

Row 4: Sl 1 purlwise wyb, [sl 1, k1] 14 (16, 14, 16, 22) times, ssk, turn.

Repeat Rows 3 and 4 until 1 gusset st rem on each side.

Leg Chart, Sizes S and L

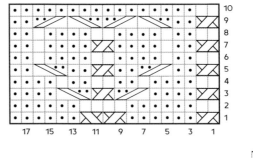

Leg Chart, Sizes XS, M, and XL

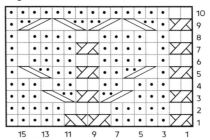

☐	knit
•	purl
⧅	1/1 RC*
⧄	1/1 LC*
⬲	1/2 RPC*
⬱	1/2 LPC*
☐	pattern repeat

* see stitch guide

Work Row 3 again, but do not turn. At this point you will resume working in the rnd.

Next Rnd: Work instep in patt as set, k2tog, rm indicating the edge of the gusset sts, k to EOR—64 (72, 80, 90, 96) sts.

Next Rnd: Work next rnd of instep patt across instep sts, work heel texture patt as established to EOR.

Cont in patt as set until you hit Rnd 31 (31, 41, 41, 41) or 41 (41, 51, 51, 51) of the instep patt, whichever comes first.

LEG

If you just completed row 41 (41, 51, 51, 51) of the instep patt, adjust the start of rnd as follows: Break yarn leaving a long enough tail to weave in ends, sl

8 (10, 8, 10, 8) sts purlwise. This is the new BOR; rejoin yarn here.

If you just completed row 31 (31, 41, 41, 41) of the instep patt, no adjustment is needed.

Leg Rnd: Work appropriate size Leg Chart 4 (4, 5, 5, 6) times around.

Work as set until Leg Chart is complete. Break working yarn, leaving a long enough tail to weave in ends, sl 8 (10, 8, 10, 8) sts purlwise. This is the new BOR; rejoin yarn here. Begin again at Rnd 1 of leg patt.

Work leg patt as set, moving the BOR before Rnd 1 each time, until sock is 2" (5 cm) less than desired length—for sizes XS, S, M, XL, end on Rnd 10 of the leg patt; for size L only, end with Rnd 9.

Size L Only

Final Rnd: K1, k1f&b, (p16, k2) 2 times, p16, k1, k1f&b, p16, k2, p16 —92 sts total.

CUFF

All Sizes

Rnd 1: [1/1 RC, p2] around.

Rnd 2: [K2, p2] around.

Repeat Rnds 1 and 2 until cuff measures 2" (5 cm), ending with Rnd 2.

BO loosely using Jeny's Surprisingly Stretchy Bind-Off (see Glossary).

finishing

To block, simply wash the socks. Weave in ends once dry.

ABOUT THE DESIGNER

Nicole Wagenblast, an avid knitter from central New Jersey, was the #operationsockdrawer winner on Episode 343 of The Knitmore Girls Podcast after posting a photo of a sock sporting a pair of aviator sunglasses. She works at Princeton University, where she can often be found knitting— surprise, surprise—and teaching others to knit. Despite having knit countless socks, her Love Needs a Heart design has the distinction of being Nicole's first published pattern and her first pair ever completed toe-up.

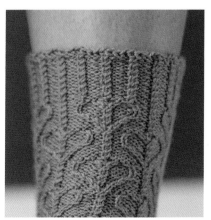

SYMMETRICAL MOSAIC COLORWORK, simple stripes, and contrasting heels, toes, and cuffs shine in this pattern. Inspired by berry-laden trees and ornate, vintage carousels, these socks feature a botanical motif, arch shaping, and easy-to-track gusset and heel flap construction. Asymmetric toes are shaped to promote comfort, but they also stretch evenly and minimize colorwork distortion, showing off your stitches to the best effect.

WORKED TOE-UP WITH A GUSSET & HEEL FLAP.

Finished Size

XS (S, M, L, XL)

Sock's foot circumference: 4½ (5½, 6½, 7½, 8¾)" (11.5 [14, 16.5, 19, 22] cm) to be worn with ½" negative ease.

Yarn

Fingering Weight (#1 Super Fine).

Shown here: Skein Top Draw Sock (85% superwash Merino, 15% nylon; 437 yd [400 m]/3½ oz [100 g]): Highlands (MC), Velvet (CC1), Freshwater Pearl (CC2), 1 hank each.

Needles

Size U.S. 0 (2 mm): Your preferred configuration for small circumference in the round: DPNs, long circular for magic loop, 2 shorter circulars, set of three flexible DPNs, 8-9" (20-23 cm) circular.

Adjust needle sizes if necessary to obtain the correct gauge (see Notes).

Notions

Removable stitch markers (optional); yarn needle.

Gauge

36 stitches and 60 rnds = 4" (10 cm) in both slip-stitch colorwork.

Notes

■ It may be helpful to switch to a larger sized needle—e.g., U.S. 1 (2.25 mm)—to work the top of foot once slip-stitch colorwork begins, to maintain gauge and assist in keeping slipped floats loose in the finished project. Working with DPNs or two circulars makes this easy.

STITCH GUIDE

KFSB (Knit Front Slip Back): Knit into the next st, but leave it on the left needle; insert tip of right needle into the back leg of the st knitwise, and slip it to the right needle.

lillipillies

— LYNNETTE HULSE —

socks
TOE (BOTH SOCKS)

Using Judy's Magic Cast-On (see Glossary) and MC, CO 14 (18, 22, 28, 32) sts.

Distribute sts or pm so that you can identify the midpoint of the rnd. The first half of the sts form the instep; the rem are the sole.

Rnd 1: Knit.

Rnd 2: K1, M1L, k to last stitch of first side, M1R, k2, M1L, k to last st, M1R, k1—4 sts inc'd.

Repeat Rnd 2 twice more—26 (30, 34, 40, 44) sts.

RIGHT TOE ONLY

Rnd 1: K to 1 st before end of instep, M1L, k2, M1R, k to EOR—2 sts inc'd.

Repeat Rnd 1 twice more—32 (36, 40, 46, 50) sts; 16 (18, 20, 23, 25) sts each on instep and sole.

Rnd 4: Knit.

Rnd 5: Repeat Rnd 1.

Repeat Rnds 4 and 5 [2 (4, 7, 8, 11)] more times—38 (46, 56, 64, 74) sts; 19 (23, 28, 32, 27) sts each on instep and sole.

Do not break yarn. Proceed to Foot.

LEFT TOE ONLY

Rnd 1: K1, M1R, k to last st, M1L, k1—2 sts inc'd.

Repeat Rnd 1 twice more—32 (36, 40, 46, 50) sts; 16 (18, 20, 23, 25) sts each on instep and sole.

Rnd 4: Knit.

Rnd 5: Repeat Rnd 1.

Lillipillies Chart, Size XS

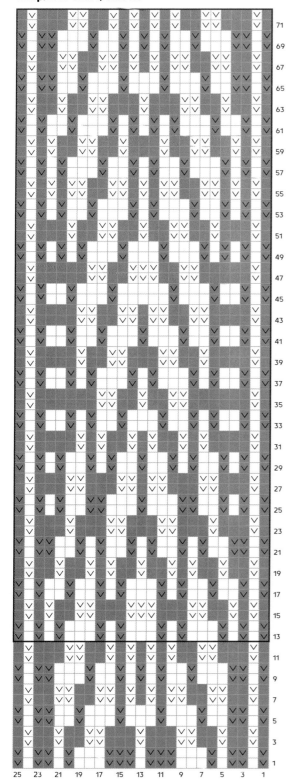

Lillipillies Chart, Size S

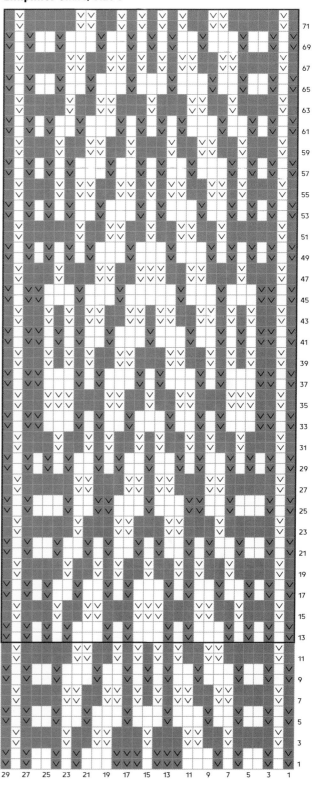

■ knit with CC1　　□ knit with CC2　　☑ sl st with color indicated　　□ pattern repeat

Lillipillies Chart, Size M

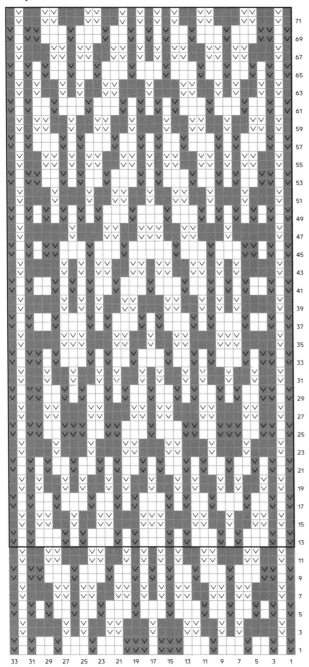

Lillipillies Chart, Size L

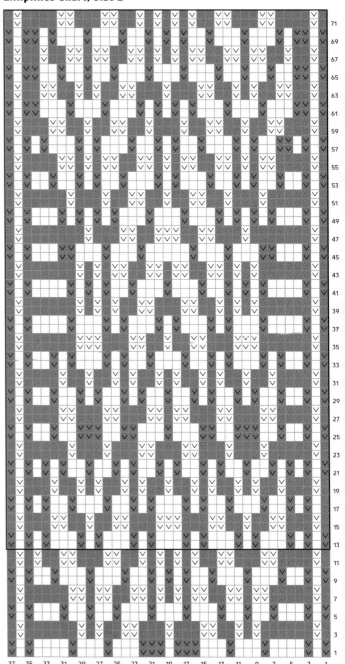

knit with CC1   knit with CC2   ⱱ sl st with color indicated   pattern repeat

Lillipillies Chart, Size XL

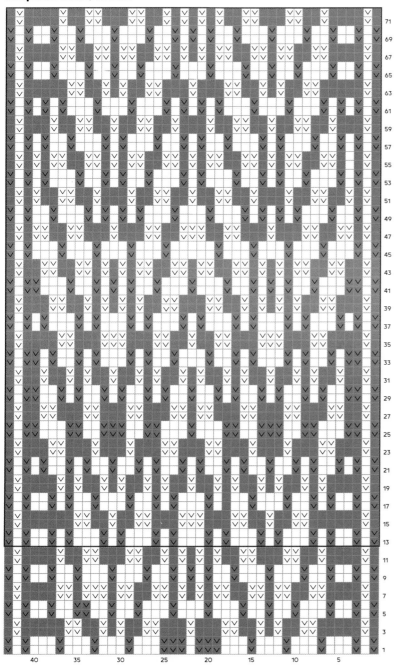

Repeat Rnds 4 and 5 [2 (4, 7, 8, 11)] more times—38 (46, 56, 64, 74) sts; 19 (23, 28, 32, 27) sts each on instep and sole.

Do not break yarn. Proceed to Foot.

FOOT

SETUP FOR COLORWORK

Rnd 1: K20 (24, 29, 33, 38)—this is the end of instep, rearrange sts or pm as desired; k17 (21, 26, 30, 35)—this is the EOR. Slip rem st to start of Rnd 21 (25, 30, 34, 39) sts for instep; 17 (21, 26, 30, 35) sts for sole.

Break MC, leaving a long tail for weaving in.

Join CC1.

Rnd 2: Knit.

Join CC2.

Rnd 3: With CC2, knit.

Rnd 4: With CC2, p across instep, k to EOR.

Rnd 5: With CC1, knit.

Rnd 6: K1, M1R, [k6 (8, 14, 16, 11), KFSB (see Stitch Guide)] 2 (2, 1, 1, 2) times, k to last st of instep, M1L, k to EOR—42 (50, 59, 67, 78) sts; 25 (29, 33, 37, 43) sts for instep; 17 (21, 26, 30, 35) sts for sole.

BEGIN COLORWORK CHARTS

Note: Consider switching to a larger needle for instep stitches only at this point.

Foot Rnd: Work Lillipillies Chart for appropriate size across instep; k to EOR.

Cont as set, changing colors every 2 rnds as indicated in the chart, until piece is approximately 3¼ (3¾, 4, 4½,

5¼)" (8.5 [9.5, 10, 11.5, 13.5] cm) shorter than required foot length, ending with a second rnd of either CC1 or CC2. Once Rnd 72 of the chart is complete, repeat Rnds 13-72.

SHAPE ARCH
For Sizes XS, S, and XL Only

Rnd 1: Work Lillipillies Chart as set across instep, k1, [sl 1, k1] to EOR.

For Sizes M and L Only

Rnd 1: Work Lillipillies Chart as set across instep, [k1, sl 1] – (–, 7, 8, –) times, k2tog, [sl 1, k1] to EOR— – (–, 25, 29, –) sts for sole.

All Sizes

Rnd 2: Work Lillipillies Chart as set across instep, k1, [sl 1, k1] to EOR.

Rnds 3 and 4: Work Lillipillies Chart as set across instep, [sl 1, k1] to last st, sl 1.

Rnds 5 and 6: Repeat Rnd 2.

Repeat Rnds 3-6 until arch shaping measures approximately ¾" (2 cm).

Next Rnd: Work Lillipillies Chart as set across instep, k to EOR.

Last Rnd of Arch Shaping: Work Lillipillies Chart as set across instep, k8 (10, 12, 14, 17) sts, KFSB, k to EOR—18 (22, 26, 30, 36) sts for sole.

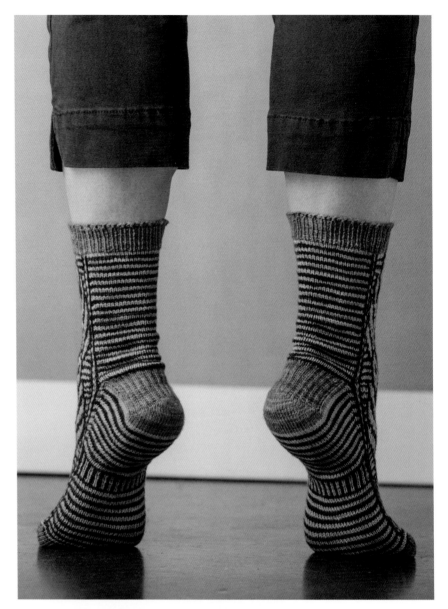

GUSSET

Rnd 1: Work Lillipillies Chart as set across instep, k to EOR.

Rnd 2: Work Lillipillies Chart as set across instep, k1, M1R, k to last st, M1L, k1—2 sts inc'd.

Repeat Rnds 1 and 2 [11 (13, 15, 17, 21)] more times—42 (50, 58, 66, 80) sts on the sole, 67 (79, 91, 103, 123) sts total.

HEEL TURN

Turn, and work across sole sts only. Join MC.

Row 1: (WS) P across sole sts, turn.

Row 2: (RS) Sl 1 wyb, k to last 12 (14, 16, 18, 22) sts, turn.

Row 3: DS (see Glossary), p to last 12 (14, 16, 18, 22) sts, turn.

Row 4: DS, k to previous DS, turn.

Row 5: DS, p to previous DS, turn.

Repeat Rows 4 and 5 until there are 6 (6, 6, 8, 10) sts between DS. Do not turn after last row.

HEEL FLAP

Row 1: (RS) K to last DS, knitting into both legs of DS, k2tog tbl on last DS and first gusset, turn.

Row 2: (WS) Sl 1 wyf, p to last DS, purling into both legs of DS, p2tog on last DS and first gusset, turn.

Row 3: [Sl 1 wyb, k1] 8 (10, 12, 14, 17) times, sl 1, k2tog tbl, turn.

Row 4: Sl 1 wyf, p16 (20, 24, 28, 34), p2tog, turn.

Repeat Rows 3 and 4 until 1 MC gusset st rem on each side of the gap.

Next Row: [Sl1, k1] to 2 sts before turn gap, sl 1, k2tog tbl, do not turn. Break MC leaving a long tail for weaving in—44 (52, 60, 68, 80) sts total.

LEG

Resume working in the rnd.

Rnd 1: Work Lillipillies Chart as set across instep, k2tog, k to EOR—43 (51, 59, 67, 79) sts.

Rnd 2: Work Lillipillies Chart as set across instep, k to EOR.

Cont with Rnd 2, until leg measures 2½ (3½, 4½, 5½, 6½)" (6 [9, 11.5, 14, 16.5] cm) or desired leg length before cuff. Break CC1 and CC2, leaving long tails for weaving in.

CUFF

Join MC. If using a larger needle for instep, change to smaller size.

Rnd 1: Knit.

Rnd 2: [K6 (8, 17, 20, 13), k2tog] 5 (5, 3, 3, 5) times, k to EOR—38 (46, 56, 64, 74) sts.

Rnd 3: [K1, p1] around.

Repeat Rnd 3 until cuff measures 1 (1, 1½, 1½, 1½)" (2.5 [2.5, 3.5, 3.5, 3.5] cm).

Bind off loosely with your preferred stretchy method.

finishing

To block, simply wash the socks. Weave in ends once dry.

ABOUT THE DESIGNER

Lynnette "Nett" Hulse is a freelance knitwear designer. The Australian mum to two delightfully spirited daughters finds designing for them and her husband endlessly inspiring. With yarn her only vice, she loves customizing everything and combines practicality with a generous dash of whimsy. She has published designs in Interweave publications, Knit Picks, Malabrigo Yarn, and the online magazine Twist Collective. Follow her yarn-related exploits on Instagram @vintagenettles; find her designs on Ravelry as Lynnette Hulse.

— ETHAN LYN —

tolstoy's triumphant thermals

WAR AND PEACE describes the governess Anna Makárovna as having a secret process for knitting two stockings at the same time on the same needles. Upon finishing them, she ceremoniously pulls one out of the other in the children's presence—two socks knit at the same time, one nested inside the other. These socks are designed as a deliberate, but hopefully still fun, challenge. Worried about making a mistake? Stick a hand in between the socks and feel around. Tolstoy doesn't mention it, but Makárovna probably did that when the kids weren't looking.

WORKED TOP DOWN, TWO-AT-A-TIME WITH A DOUBLE KNITTING METHOD. AFTERTHOUGHT HEEL & A CINCHED WEDGE TOE.

Finished Size

XS (S, M, L, XL)

Sock's foot circumference: 7 (7½, 8, 8½, 9)" (18 [19, 20.5, 21.5, 23] cm).

Choose a size with approximately 1" (2.5 cm) negative ease in the foot circumference.

Yarn

Fingering weight (#1 Super Fine).

Shown here: Urth Yarns Uneek Sock (75% extrafine superwash Merino, 25% nylon; 220 yd [200 m]/1¾ oz [50 g]): #60, 2 balls.

Needles

Size U.S. 1 (2.25 mm): Your preferred configuration for small circumference in the round: DPNs, long circular for magic loop, 2 shorter circulars, set of three flexible DPNs, 8-9" (20-23 cm) circular.

A second set of needles in a similar size for use as stitch holders (optional; stitch holders or waste yarn can also be used).

Adjust needle sizes if necessary to obtain the correct gauge.

Notions

Waste yarn; cable needle; yarn needle; locking stitch markers for fixing errors.

Gauge

32 sts and 46 rnds = 4" (10 cm) in double-knit stockinette st.

32 sts and 49 rnds = 4" (10 cm) in double-knit thermal patt.

double-knitting techniques

Double-knitting consists of two layers of fabric constructed simultaneously. Most double-knitting patterns create one reversible item by connecting the layers, but in this pattern, the yarns never cross. This means the two layers never connect and can be completely separated at the end.

Double-checking the cast-on
To ensure that your strands haven't crossed, slide the lines of stitches from underneath the needle apart, bringing yarn A toward you and yarn B away from you. Your cast-ons should be separate but fit together like gears, or the teeth of a zipper.

How to double-knit knit and purl stitches
Where the yarns are held while knitting is critical. Yarn A is for working the outside sock, and yarn B for the inside sock; hold them as follows:

- For a knit stitch on the outside layer, hold both yarns at the back.
- For a knit stitch on the inside layer, hold yarn A at the front, yarn B at the back.
- For a purl stitch on the outside layer, hold yarn A at the front, yarn B at the back.
- For a purl stitch on the inside layer, hold both yarns at the front.

Another way to think about it:

- Yarn A is always held at the front so it doesn't cross yarn B, unless it needs to be in back to knit that stitch.
- Yarn B is always held at the back so it doesn't cross yarn A, unless it needs to be in front to purl that stitch.

Notes

- The thermal pattern combines stockinette st with the same ribbing from the cuffs, and the toes and heels are cinched together at the end, which means no grafting. The afterthought heels are worked as a little break from the feet (mid-thought heels, in a way), so closing the toes comes at the very end.

- The outside sock is worked in yarn A; the inside sock in yarn B. Offsetting the stripe repeats (working yarn A and yarn B in different colors) helps to differentiate between the two socks, making it easier to spot errors and keep the yarns from crossing.

- While knitting, the right sides of each layer are facing you, and the sts on the needles alternate one-by-one between layers.

- Yarn A should always be in front of yarn B to prevent the yarns from crossing—every time you drop the yarns and pick them back up, double-check to make sure you haven't twisted them.

- Afterthought heel setup consists of 2 rows of flat knitting in waste yarn (not double-knit) that are unraveled, with lifelines in the sts directly above and below to aid in picking up two layers of sts.

STITCH GUIDE
Yarn A is always held in front of yarn B.

Double-knit Stockinette Stitch (2 st repeat):
- With both yarns held at back of work, knit a st of outside sock with yarn A. Move yarn A to front.
- Knit a st of inside sock with yarn B. Move yarn A to back.

Double-knit 1×1 Ribbing (4 st repeat):

- With both yarns held at back of work, knit a st on outside sock with yarn A. Move yarn A to front.

- Knit a st of inside sock with yarn B.

- Purl a st of outside sock with yarn A. Move yarn B to front.

- With both yarns held at front, purl a st of inside sock with yarn B. Move both yarns to back.

Double-knit Thermal Pattern (4 st, 3 rnd repeat):

- **Rnds 1 and 2:** Work in double-knit stockinette st.

- **Rnd 3:** Work in double-knit 1×1 ribbing.

Double-knit ssk (dk-ssk) or sssk (dk-sssk):

Slip 1 st (yarn A) to right needle, *use cable needle to hold next st (yarn B) at back. Slip next st (yarn A) to right needle*, return st(s) on cable needle to left needle, slip yarn A sts back to left needle. Ssk in yarn A, ssk in yarn B—2 sts decreased (1 per sock).

- Work dk-sssk as above, but working steps between asterisks twice. Sssk in yarn A, sssk in yarn B—4 sts decreased (2 per sock).

Double-knit k2tog (dk-k2tog) or k3tog (dk-k3tog):

Slip 1 (yarn A) to right needle, *use cable needle to hold next st (yarn B) at back. Slip next st (yarn A) to right needle*, return st(s) on cable needle to left needle, slip yarn A sts back to left needle. K2tog in A, k2tog in yarn B—2 sts decreased (1 per sock).

- Work dk-k3tog as above, but working steps between asterisks twice. K3tog in yarn A, k3tog in yarn B—4 sts decreased (2 per sock).

socks

SETUP YARNS

Wind off one color repeat from the end of yarn A (about 12 g); set aside for heel of outside sock. Wind off an equal amount from the beginning of yarn B; set aside for heel of inside sock.

Using your preferred stretchy method, CO 56 (60, 64, 68, 72) sts in each color, onto separate needles. Hold the needles so that the yarn A stitches (and their yarn) are in front, and the yarn B stitches (and their yarn) are in back. Using the working needle, join them as follows: slip a yarn A stitch onto the working needle, slip a yarn B stitch onto the working needle, and cont, until all stitches have been merged. Each needle should start with a yarn A stitch, and end with a yarn B stitch.

Distribute sts across needles as you prefer and join for working in the round. Note or mark start of round as required.

CUFF

Work double-knit 1x1 ribbing (see Stitch Guide) for 2¼" (5.5 cm).

LEG

Work in double-knit thermal pattern (see Stitch Guide) until piece measures about 6¼" (16 cm), ending after Rnd 1 of thermal patt.

SETUP AFTER-THOUGHT HEELS

Using a yarn needle, thread a 12" (30 cm) strand of waste yarn through the first 56 (60, 64, 68, 72) sts of the rnd, (28 [30, 32, 34, 36] sts per sock), leaving the sts on the circular needle. Drop waste yarn. With a 9' (3 m) length of waste yarn, work flat, back and forth in a single layer across the same 56 (60, 64, 68, 72) sts for 2 rows, ending back at the start of the rnd. This joins the socks, but this yarn will be removed, and the socks separated when it's time to work the heel. Cut waste yarn.

Resuming using yarns A and B and double-knit stockinette stitch (see Stitch Guide), work 56 (60, 64, 68, 72) sts. Using a yarn needle, thread another 12" (30 cm) strand of waste yarn through the 56 (60, 64, 68, 72) sts just worked, leaving the sts on the circular needle. Using yarns A and B, cont working to the EOR.

FEET

Foot Rnd: Work across sole sts—56 (60, 64, 68, 72) sts total, 28 (30, 32, 34, 36) per sock—in double-knit stockinette, work across instep sts—56 (60, 64, 68, 72) sts total, 28 (30, 32, 34, 36) per sock—in double-knit thermal patt, beg with Rnd 3. Work until piece measures approximately 3" (7.5 cm) past the heel setup—it doesn't need to be too precise.

Slip the working stitches to spare needles or waste yarn for holders. You'll use the active needles to work the heel.

HEELS

Unravel 2 rows of waste yarn at heel gap. Using the now-empty needles, pick up (don't knit) sts from the two lengths of waste yarn: 56 (60, 64, 68, 72) sts from the leg (28 [30, 32, 34, 36] per sock), one st of each A and B across the gap, pm, 58 (62, 66, 70, 74) sts from the sole (29 [31, 33, 35, 37] per sock), pm to mark end of rnd, and one st of each A and B across the gap. Last two gap sts picked up are beg of rnd—60 (64, 68, 72, 76) sts (30 [32, 34, 36, 38] per sock) on the leg side of heel; 58 (62, 66, 70, 74) sts (29 [31, 33, 35, 37] per sock) on the sole side; 118 (126, 134, 142, 150) total sts (59 [63, 67, 71, 75] total sts per sock). Distribute sts and pm as required so that you can identify the break between the leg and sole side stitches.

Using the small balls of yarns A and B set aside earlier—yarn A for the outside sock, yarn B for the inside sock—work double-knit stockinette in the rnd until heel measures 1¼" (3 cm).

Setup Rnd: Work 2 sts in double-knit stockinette (1 per sock), dk-ssk (see Stitch Guide), work in double-knit stockinette to 6 sts (3 per sock) before end of leg sts, dk-k2tog (see Stitch Guide), work 4 sts in double-knit stockinette (2 per sock), dk-ssk, work in double-knit stockinette to EOR—112 (120, 128, 136, 144) sts, (56 [60, 64, 68, 72] per sock).

fixing errors

Accidentally attaching the socks to each other can be prevented!

- Check frequently to make sure the socks fully separate. Insert your hand to physically check or look at the inside and outside of the work: yarn A should only be visible on the outside sock and yarn B on the inside sock.

- If the strands do get crossed: find the problem st(s), drop down to the mistake, separate the two layers, and ladder each column of sts back up. If sock B has an error that's difficult to fix

from the visible side (WS), drop a few sock A sts down a few rows, hold them on a locking stitch marker, fix sock B, and ladder sock A sts back up. Rearrange the sts in alternating A/B order before continuing.

- If there's an error where yarns A and B are similar colors, determine if yarns A and B were crossed, as above, or if which yarn is A and which is B were switched. For the latter, the only solution is to unknit back to the mistake and reknit.

Next Rnd, dec 4 per sock: Work 2 sts in double-knit stockinette (1 per sock), dk-ssk, work in double-knit stockinette to 6 sts (3 per sock) before end of leg sts, dk-k2tog, work 4 sts in double-knit stockinette (2 per sock), dk-ssk, work in double-knit stockinette to 6 sts (3 per sock) before EOR, dk-k2tog, work in double-knit stockinette to EOR—4 sts dec'd.

Repeat the last rnd 6 (7, 8, 9, 10) more times—24 sts rem (12 per sock).

Next Rnd, dec 8 per sock: Work 2 sts in double-knit stockinette (1 per sock), dk-sssk, work in double-knit stocki-nette to 8 sts (4 per sock) before end of leg sts, dk-k3tog, work 4 sts in double-knit stockinette (2 per sock), dk-sssk, work in double-knit stockinette to 8 sts (4 per sock) before EOR, dk-k3tog, work in double-knit stockinette to EOR—8 sts dec'd.

Repeat the last rnd once more—56 sts rem (28 per sock).

Final Rnd: [Work 2 sts in double-knit stockinette (1 per sock), dk-ssk, dk-k2tog, work 2 sts in double-knit stockinette (1 per sock)] twice—16 sts rem (8 per sock).

To cinch heels closed, cut yarns A and B, leaving 12" (30 cm) tails. Thread tail of yarn B onto yarn needle. Working clockwise, thread tail through back legs of all yarn B sts; don't pull tight. Thread yarn needle and tail through the center hole so tail of yarn B rests on the inside of the socks. Thread tail of yarn A onto yarn needle. Working clockwise, thread tail through the front legs of all yarn A sts; don't pull tight. Tail of yarn A rests on the outside of the socks. Remove all sts from needles; pull both tails tight to cinch and separate the heels.

COMPLETE FOOT

Return stitches of foot from holders/spare needles to working needles.

Cont working sole and instep sts as set until foot from back of heel measures 1½ (1½, 1¾, 2, 2)" (3.8 [3.8, 4.5, 5, 5] cm) less than desired foot length, ending after Rnd 3 of the thermal patt.

TOES

Dec Rnd: Work 2 sts in double-knit stockinette (1 per sock), dk-ssk, work in double-knit stockinette to 6 sts (3 per sock) before end of sole sts, dk-k2tog, work 4 sts in double-knit stockinette

(2 per sock), dk-ssk, work in double-knit stockinette to 6 sts (3 per sock) before EOR, dk-k2tog, work in double-knit stockinette to EOR—4 sts dec'd.

Work 1 rnd even in double-knit stockinette.

Rep the last two rnds 5 (6, 6, 7, 7) more times—64 (64, 72, 72, 80) sts (32 [32, 36, 36, 40] per sock).

Work Dec Rnd 6 (6, 7, 7, 8) times—16 sts rem (8 sts per sock).

Cinch closed as for heels.

finishing

Take sock B out of sock A—trium-phantly, if desired!

To block, simply wash the socks. Weave in ends once dry.

ABOUT THE DESIGNER

Ethan is a queer and transgender knitter, songwriter, and Russophile living in Chicago. They listen to the Knitmore Girls with their partner, who also knits, and the two have an unspoken rule that neither of them can listen to a new episode in the other's absence. Ethan's currently working on their second drawer of hand-knit socks and does a lot of double-knitting because when they try stranded colorwork, their floats are always too tight.

WHEN SHE BEGAN snowboarding many years ago, Felicia fell in love with ski socks—socks that are durable, thick, and cushy without being bulky, and that hug the insole of your foot. She wears ski socks even when not on the mountain because she loves the fit and feel that much. Felicia finally decided it was time to knit a pair of cozy ski socks not for skiing or snowboarding but just for lounging around the house after a day in the snow. This pattern knits up quickly in worsted gauge with a doubled-up, nylon-reinforced sock yarn for the toes and heels. It features a textured Eye of Partridge slip-stitch pattern in the middle of the foot in order to produce that foot-hugging fit. The leg of the sock is finished off in a fun two-color brioche rib that gives these socks a quirky and retro legwarmer look.

WORKED TOE-UP WITH
AN AFTERTHOUGHT,
SHORT-ROW HEEL.

Finished Size
XS (S, M, L, XL)

Sock's foot circumference: 7 (7½, 8¼, 9, 9½)" (18 [19, 21, 23, 24] cm) to be worn with about 1" (2.5 cm) negative ease.

Yarn
Worsted weight (#4 Medium).

Shown here: SweetGeorgia Yarns Tough Love Sock (80% superwash Merino, 20% nylon; 425 yd [388 m]/4 oz [115 g]): Lollipop (CC1), 1 skein held double (only used about 1 oz/30 g). SweetGeorgia Yarns Superwash Worsted (100% superwash Merino; 200 yd [182 m]/4 oz [115 g]): Charcoal (MC), 2 skeins; Rainbow Sprinkles (CC2), 1 skein.

Needles
Size U.S. 3 (3.25 mm): Your preferred configuration for small circumference in the round: DPNs, long circular for magic loop, 2 shorter circulars, set of three flexible DPNs, 8-9" (20-23 cm) circular.

Adjust needle size if necessary to obtain the correct gauge.

Notions
Stitch marker; yarn needle; approx. 1 yd (1 m) of waste yarn (smooth, and should be a contrasting color).

Gauge
26 sts and 28 rnds = 4" (10 cm) in Stockinette st with yarns held double.

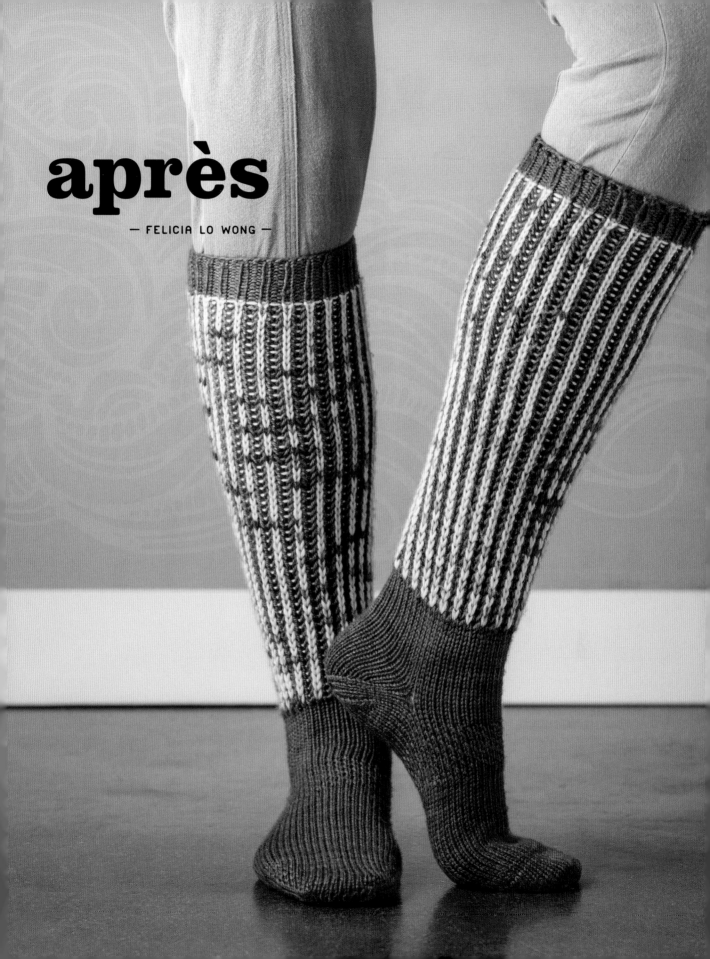

après

— FELICIA LO WONG —

STITCH GUIDE

brk (Brioche Knit): Knit next knit st together with its paired yarn over.

brp (Brioche Purl): Purl next purl st together with its paired yarn over.

YOS (slip stitch and create yarnover wrap): Make sure yarn is in front of work; on a knit rnd, you'll need to bring it to the front, on a purl rnd it will already be there. Slip the next st as if to purl, and then take the yarn over the needle into position for the next st; on a knit rnd, just let it drape over the needle to the back, on a purl rnd, bring it all the way to the front again.

socks

Using CC1, smaller needles, and Judy's Magic Cast-On (see Glossary), CO 14 (16, 18, 18, 18)—7 (8, 9, 9, 9) sts on each half of the sock. Distribute sts or pm to designate the start and midpoint of the rnd.

TOE

Rnd 1: Knit.

Rnd 2: K1, M1L, k to last st on needle, M1R, k1, sm, k1, M1L, k to last st on needle, M1R, k1—4 sts inc'd.

Repeat these last two rnds 7 (7, 8, 9, 10) more times—46 (48, 54, 58, 62) sts.

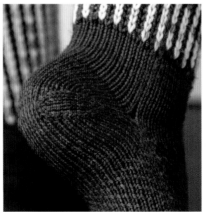

FOOT

Switch to MC.

Knit even for 2 (2¼, 2½, 3, 3½)" (5 [5.5, 6.5, 7.5, 9] cm).

SHAPE ARCH

Begin Eye of Partridge patt for arch of foot.

Rnd 1: [Sl 1 purlwise wyb, k1] around.

Rnd 2: Knit.

Rnd 3: [K1, sl 1 purlwise wyb] around.

Rnd 4: Knit.

Work Rnds 1–4 for 1¼ (1½, 1½, 1½, 1½)" (3.2 [3.8, 3.8, 3.8, 3.8] cm).

Knit all rnds until foot measures 2½ (2½, 2¾, 2¾, 2¾)" (6.5 [6.5, 7, 7, 7] cm) short of desired foot length.

SETUP FOR HEEL

K23 (24, 27, 29, 31) to midpoint of rnd, and then k the rem 23 (24, 27, 29, 31) sts with waste yarn. Slide the 23 (24, 27, 29, 31) sts just worked back onto the left needle and then k them again with the MC.

LEG

Knit even for 2" (5 cm).

Begin brioche patt as foll:

Setup Rnd 1: With MC, [YOS (see Stitch Guide), p1] around.

Leaving MC hanging at front of work, cont with CC2.

Setup Rnd 2: With CC2, [brk (see Stitch Guide), YOS] around.

Leaving CC2 hanging at back of work, cont with MC.

Rnd 3: With MC, [YOS, brp (see Stitch Guide)] around. Leave MC in front of work.

Rnd 4: With CC2, [brk, YOS] around. Leave CC2 in back of work.

Repeat Rnds 3 and 4 until brioche patt reaches 10" (25.5 cm).

Break CC2 and complete sock with MC.

Final Rnd: With MC, [k1, brp] around.

CUFF

Ribbing Rnd: [K1, p1] around.

Work ribbing as set for 1½" (4 cm) and BO as follows: K1, *k1; return the sts to the left needle without twisting and k2tog tbl; rep from * until all sts have been worked. Cut yarn and pull through final st to secure.

AFTERTHOUGHT HEEL

Unpick the waste yarn and return all the live stitches to smaller needle. Pm or distribute sts so that sts are divided at each side of foot, marking the start of rnd and halfway through the rnd.

Reattach CC1 at the side of the foot—doesn't matter which side. Knit 10 rnds.

Rnd 1, dec: K1, ssk, knit until last 3 sts before the side of foot, k2tog, k2, ssk, knit until the last 3 sts before EOR, k2tog, k1—4 sts dec'd.

Rnd 2: Knit.

Repeat Rnds 1 and 2 until 22 (24, 26, 30, 30) sts rem.

finishing

Cut yarn, leaving a 12" (30 cm) tail. Divide sts evenly across two needles, and with tail threaded on a yarn needle, use Kitchener stitch (see Glossary) to graft heel closed.

To block, simply wash the socks. Weave in ends once dry.

ABOUT THE DESIGNER

Felicia Lo Wong is a designer and entrepreneur born and raised in Vancouver, Canada. Her lifelong passion for knitting, color, and design led her to start the SweetGeorgia blog in 2004. A year later, SweetGeorgia was founded at her dining room table with nothing more than three skeins of sock yarn for sale. In 2017, Felicia published Dyeing to Spin & Knit. She's currently developing the School of SweetGeorgia to offer online fiber arts education.

a drawer full

— BECKY GREENE —

WHAT MIGHT A knitter do to take a sock-knitting obsession to a higher level? Knit socks with sock designs on them, of course! This pattern is a miniature sock drawer all on its own. Knit these socks in a beautiful gradient yarn to easily add variety to the tiny stockings, or dig out scraps of leftover sock yarn and knit a pair of socks that remind you of older, favorite projects. The stranded pattern for these socks is simple, so don't be intimidated by trying to knit with more than one color.

WORKED TOP DOWN, WITH A FLAP-AND-GUSSET HEEL & GRAFTED WEDGE TOE.

Finished Size
XS (S, M, L, XL)

Sock's foot circumference: 7 (8, 9, 10, 11)" (18 [20.5, 23, 25.5, 28] cm) to be worn with about ½" (1.5 cm) negative ease.

Yarn
Fingering weight (#1 Super Fine).

Shown here: Schoppel Zauberball (75% superwash wool, 25% polyamide; 460 yd [420 m]/3½ oz [100 g]): #1564 Light Gray (MC), 1 ball; Schoppel Wolle Jeans Ball (75% superwash wool, 25% polyamide; 437 yd [400 m]/3½ oz [100 g]): #2126 Müllers Esel (CC), 1 ball.

Needles
Size U.S. 1½ (2.5 mm): Your preferred configuration for small circumference in the round: DPNs, long circular for magic loop, 2 shorter circulars, set of three flexible DPNs, 8-9" (20-23 cm) circular.

Adjust needle size if necessary to obtain the correct gauge.

Notions
Stitch markers; yarn needle.

Gauge
36 sts and 44 rnds = 4" (10 cm) in stranded colorwork.

socks

With MC, CO 56 (64, 72, 80, 88) sts. Distribute sts across needles as you prefer and join for working in the rnd. Note or mark start of rnd as required.

CUFF

Rnds 1–15: [K2, p1, k2, p1, k1, p1] around.

Knit two rnds.

LEG

Join CC and work Rnds 1–26 of the Drawer Full Chart twice, then work Rnds 1–10 once more.

HEEL FLAP

Note: It may be helpful to place instep sts on holder while working the heel.

Next Rnd: (RS) Work Rnd 11 of Drawer Full Chart as set to last 2 (0, 2, 0, 2) sts. Turn.

Heel flap and turn are worked only in MC; leave CC attached.

Row 1: (WS) Sl 1 wyf, p27 (31, 35, 39, 43) sts.

Row 2: [Sl 1, k1] across.

Row 3: Sl 1 wyf, p across.

Repeat Rows 2 and 3 until heel flap measures 2½ (2¾, 2¾, 3, 3)" (6.5 [7, 7, 7.5, 7.5] cm).

TURN HEEL

Row 1: (RS) Sl 1 wyb, k16 (18, 20, 24, 26) sts, ssk, k1, turn.

Row 2: (WS) Sl 1 wyf, p7 (7, 7, 11, 11), p2tog, p1, turn.

Row 3: Sl 1 wyb, k to 1 st before gap, ssk, k1, turn.

Row 4: Sl 1 wyf, p to 1 st before gap, p2tog, p1, turn.

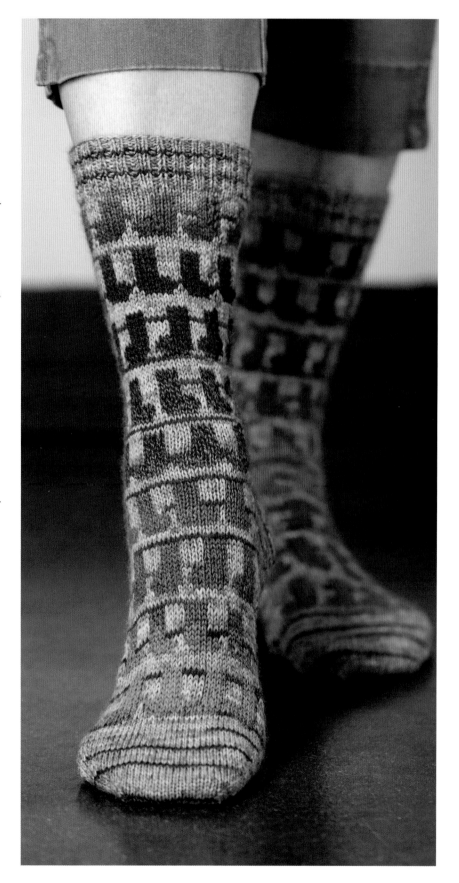

Repeat Rows 3 and 4 until all heel sts have been worked—18 (20, 22, 26, 28) sts rem.

GUSSET

Continuing with MC, k across heel sts. Pick up and knit 1 st in each sl st on edge of heel, placing a st marker after picked-up st 5 (6, 7, 7, 8) for the start of the gusset sts. The start of the instep is the new BOR; rearrange sts or pm as required. K across instep; pick up the same number of sts across 2nd side of heel flap as the first side, pm for end of gusset sts to match the first side. K to EOR.

Setup Rnd: K across instep, if the number of sts in the gusset sections is odd, k to EOR. If the number of sts is even, k1, ssk, k to last 3 sts of rnd, k2tog, k1.

Pick up CC and begin to work from charts.

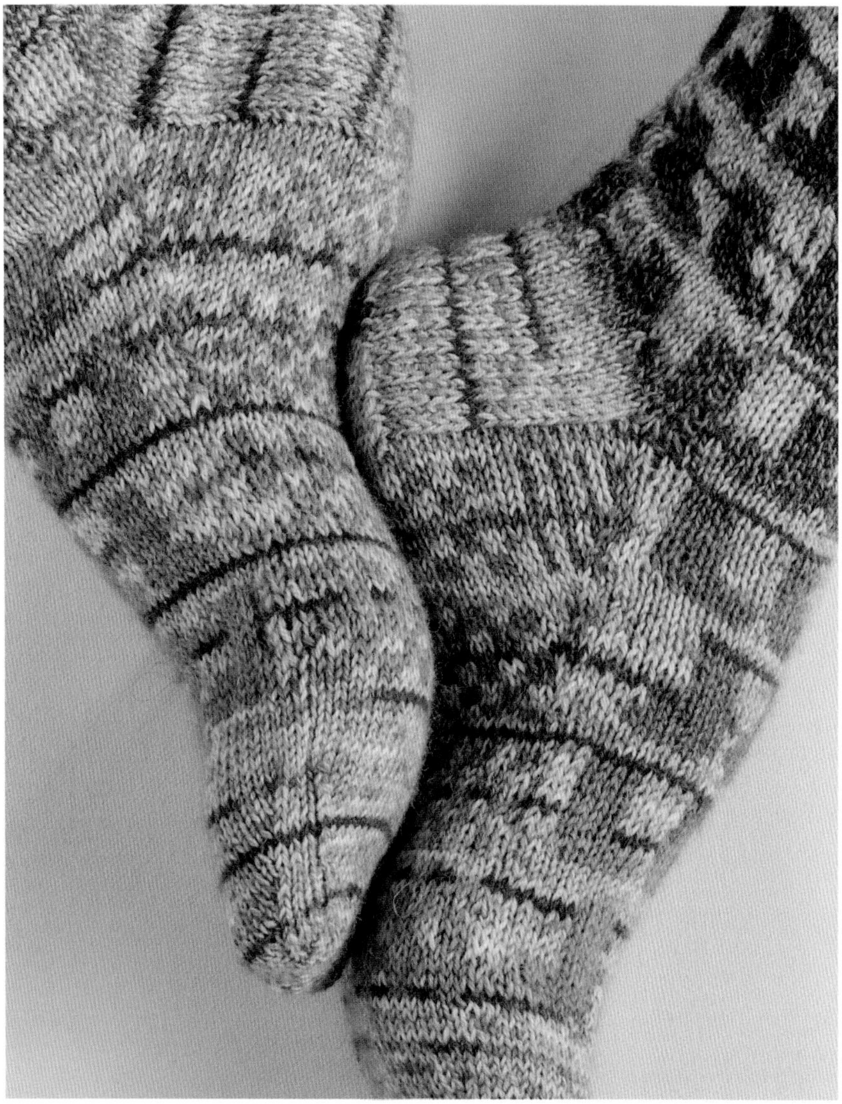

Drawer Full Chart

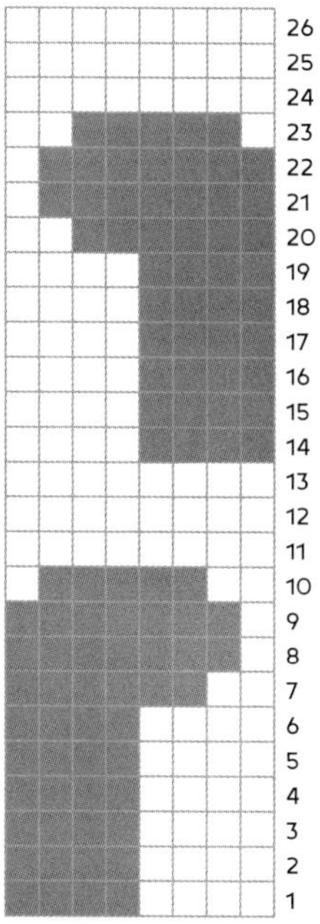

8-st patt rep

Sole Chart

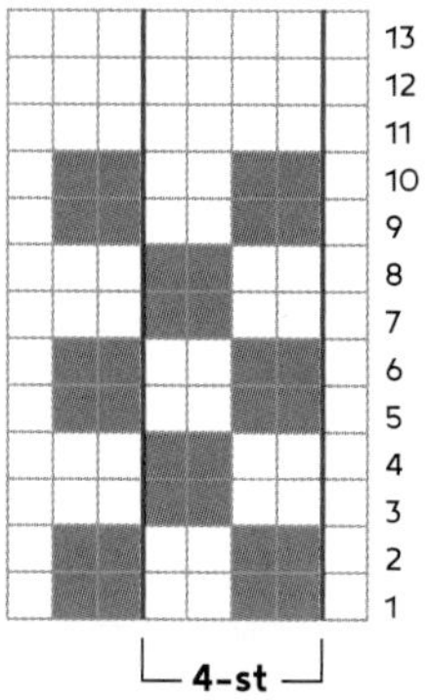

4-st patt rep

- knit with MC
- knit with CC
- pattern repeat

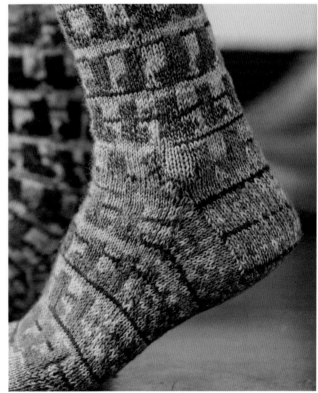

Note: When knitting across the sole, work the first st of the Sole Chart, work the 4-st repeat across to the last 3 sole sts, work the final 3 sts of chart.

Rnd 1: With MC, k2 (0, 2, 0, 2) sts; work Drawer Full Chart 3 (4, 4, 5, 5) times across instep; [k1 MC, k1 CC] to last gusset st, k1 MC; work Sole Chart across sole sts: [k1 MC, k1 CC] to last st of rnd, k1 MC.

Rnd 2: Cont in patt as set across instep; k1 MC, ssk CC, cont in stripe patt for gusset (k each color as presented); work sole patt; sm; work stripe patt to last 3 sts, k2tog CC, k1 MC—2 sts dec'd.

Rnd 3: Work even in patt as set.

Repeat Rnds 2 and 3 until 1 gusset st rem on each side.

Final Gusset Dec Rnd: Cont in patt as set across instep, ssk with MC, removing gusset marker, cont with Sole Chart starting at st 2 and work across to 2 st before EOR, remove gusset marker and k2tog with MC.

Work even in patts as set until sock is 1¾ (2, 2, 2, 2)" (4.5 [5, 5, 5, 5] cm) short of desired foot length.

Note: If necessary for correct foot length, discontinue colorwork patts early rather than cutting off in the middle of a row of the sock patt.

TOE

Rnd 1: [K1, ssk, k to last 3 sts of instep, k2tog, k1]; rep for sole

Rnd 2: Knit.

Repeat Rnds 1 and 2 until 20 (24, 32, 40, 48) sts rem.

finishing

Cut yarn, leaving a 12" (30 cm) tail. Divide sts evenly across two needles, and with tail threaded on a yarn needle, use Kitchener st to graft toe closed.

To block, simply wash the socks. Stretching on sock blockers is not required. Weave in ends once dry.

ABOUT THE DESIGNER

Becky Greene lives and knits in Washington state. She knits far too many socks for any human to ever be able to wear— she even dreams about knitting socks!—yet can't seem to squelch the compulsion. She's currently obsessed with color-work, probably in a vain attempt to use up leftover yarn. She has had several designs published in the What Would Madame Defarge Knit? book series.

saunter

— SUSIE WHITE —

THIS PATTERN INCLUDES enough details to keep you engaged while also being simple and intuitive. The socks make for great on-the-go knitting (a must for today's busy knitter) because after knitting a single repeat, the pattern is easily remembered. It's also easy to "read" on the needles, so putting the knitting down and picking it back up later is no problem at all. Between the garter stitch and traveling slip-stitches, these socks will look great in a variety of yarns, as fun to wear as they are to knit. The main stitch pattern consists of slip-stitches that travel over garter stitch by way of 1-over-1 crossed stitches framed with a ribbed column down each side of the leg. The textures continue in the Eye of Partridge heel flap, and the socks end with a rounded toe.

WORKED TOP DOWN, WITH A FLAP-AND-GUSSET HEEL & GRAFTED WEDGE TOE.

Finished Size

XS (S, M, L, XL)

Sock's foot circumference: 6¼ (6¾, 7¾, 8¾, 9¾)" (16 [17, 19.5, 22, 25] cm).

Choose a size with approximately 1" (2.5 cm) negative ease in the leg circumference.

Yarn

Fingering weight (#1 Super Fine).

Shown here: Sunshine Yarns Luxury Sock (80% superwash Merino, 10% cashmere, 10% nylon; 385 yd [352 m]/4 oz [115 g]): Moon Phase, 1 skein.

Needles

Size U.S. 1½ (2.5 mm): Your preferred configuration for small circumference in the round: DPNs, long circular for magic loop, 2 shorter circulars, set of three flexible DPNs, 8-9" (20-23 cm) circular.

Adjust needle size if necessary to obtain the correct gauge.

Notions

Stitch marker; cable needle; yarn needle.

Gauge

32 sts and 48 rnds = 4" (10 cm) in Stockinette st.

STITCH GUIDE

1/1 LC: Slip 1 st to cable needle and hold in front of work; k1; k1 from cable needle.

1/1 RC: Slip 1 st to cable needle and hold in back of work; k1; k1 from cable needle.

socks

CO 50 (54, 62, 70, 78) sts. Distribute sts across needles as you prefer and join for working in the rnd. Note or mark start of rnd as required.

CUFF

Cuff Rnd: Work Ribbing Rnd as per appropriate size Saunter Chart twice around.

Work ribbing as set until piece measures 1½" (4 cm) from cast-on, or desired length.

LEG

Leg Rnd: Starting with Rnd 1, work appropriate size chart twice around.

Work chart Rnds 1–12 until leg measures 4¼ (5, 6¼, 7¼, 7¾)" (11 [12.5, 16, 18.5, 19.5] cm) from cast-on edge, or desired length, ending with an even-numbered rnd.

HEEL FLAP

The heel flap will be worked back and forth over the next 25 (27, 31, 35, 39) sts. The rem 25 (27, 31, 35, 39) sts are the instep sts.

Row 1: (WS) K3, [sl 1, k1] to last 2 sts, k2.

Row 2: K3, p to last 3 sts, k3.

Row 3: K3, [k1, sl 1] to last 4 sts, k1, k3.

Row 4: Repeat Row 2.

Repeat Rows 1–4 until heel flap measures 2 (2, 2¼, 2¼, 2½)" (5 [5, 5.5, 5.5, 6.5] cm), or desired length, ending after a WS row.

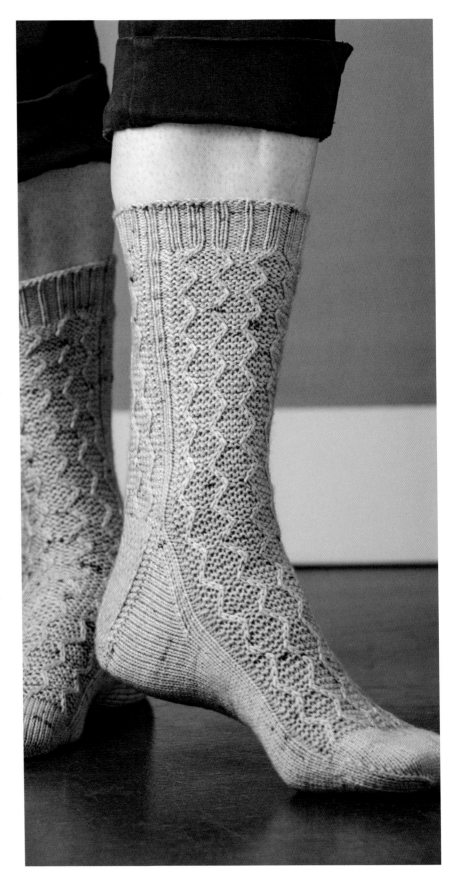

Saunter Chart, Size XS

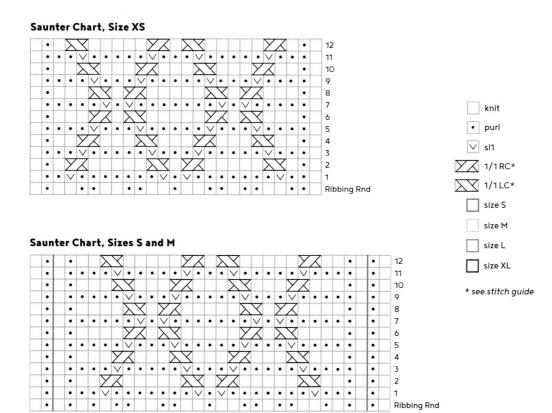

Saunter Chart, Sizes S and M

Saunter Chart, Sizes L and XL

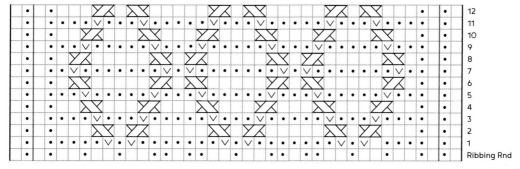

knit

· purl

∨ sl1

1/1 RC*

1/1 LC*

size S

size M

size L

size XL

see stitch guide

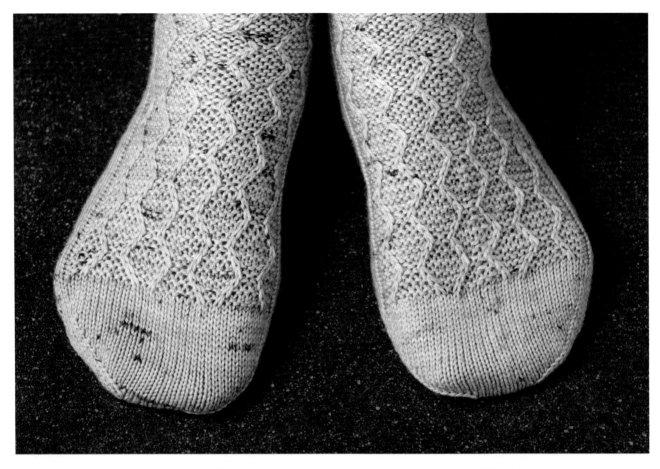

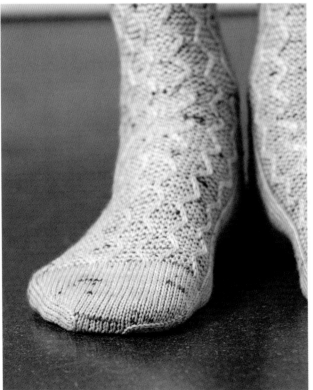

HEEL TURN

Row 1: (RS) K14 (16, 18, 20, 22), ssk, k1, turn.

Row 2: (WS) Sl 1 wyf, p4 (6, 6, 6, 6), p2tog, p1, turn.

Row 3: Sl 1 wyb, k to 1 st before gap, ssk, k1, turn.

Row 4: Sl 1 wyf, p to 1 st before gap, p2tog, p1, turn.

Repeat Rows 3 and 4 until 15 (17, 19, 21, 23) heel sts rem.

GUSSET

Setup Rnd: K across rem heel sts, then pick up and knit 1 st in each garter ridge along edge of heel flap. Work across instep in patt as set. Pick up and knit 1 st in each garter ridge along edge of heel flap; 8 (9, 10, 11, 12) sts to center of heel. This is the new EOR; pm or rearrange sts as you prefer.

Gusset Rnd 1: K to instep; work across instep in patt as set; k to EOR.

Gusset Rnd 2: K to 3 sts before instep, k2tog, k1; work instep in patt as set; k1, ssk, k to EOR—2 sts dec'd.

Repeat Gusset Rnds 1 and 2 until 56 (60, 64, 72, 78) sts rem.

FOOT

Work even, with instep sts in patt and sole sts in St st as set until foot measures 2" (5 cm) less than desired total foot length.

TOE

Rearrange sts evenly between needles. K8 (8, 7, 5, 4) rnds even.

Rnd 1: K to 3 sts before start of instep sts, k2tog, k2, ssk, k to 3 sts before end of instep sts, k2tog, k2, ssk, k to EOR—4 sts dec'd.

Knit 2 rnds.

Repeat the last 3 rnds once more.

Next Rnd: Repeat Rnd 1.

Next Rnd: Knit.

Repeat the last 2 rnds twice.

Repeat Rnd 1 until 14 (18, 22, 22, 26) total sts rem.

Setup for closure: K to start of instep sts.

finishing

Cut yarn, leaving a 12" (30 cm) tail. With tail threaded on a yarn needle, use Kitchener stitch (see Glossary) to graft toe closed.

To block, simply wash the socks. Weave in ends once dry.

ABOUT THE DESIGNER

Susie White taught herself to knit in 2006, and it has consumed her free time ever since. She started designing on a lark in order to use variegated yarn in projects other than plain socks but quickly discovered she enjoys the challenge and process of designing as much as she does knitting. She currently knits and designs in eastern Nebraska, where, in order to legitimize her near-constant thinking and talking about knitting, she also co-hosts the Prairie Girls Knit and Spin audio podcast. Find her on Ravelry and Instagram as @prairiegirlsusie. Email her at prairiegirlsusie@gmail.com.

abbreviations

The following are the most common abbreviations that appear in this book. For other terms, be sure to check individual pattern stitch guides. For more advanced techniques, see the Glossary or see Interweave's online glossary at www.interweave.com/interweave-knitting-glossary for more information.

beg(s) begin(s); beginning

BO bind-off

BOR beginning of round/row

CC contrast color

cdd central double decrease; slip 2 stitches at the same time knitwise, k1, pass the 2 slipped sts over st just knit

cm centimeter(s)

CO cast-on

cont continue(s); continuing

dec(s)('d) decrease(s); decreasing; decreased

dpn double-pointed needles

DS double stitch (German short-row, see Glossary)

EOR end of round/row

foll follow(s); following

g gram(s)

inc(s)('d) increase(s); increasing; increase(d)

k knit

k1f&b knit into the front and back of the same stitch (increase)

k2tog knit 2 stitches together (decrease)

k3tog knit 3 stitches together (decrease)

LLI (left lifted increase) pick up the left leg of the stitch 2 rows/rounds below the stitch just worked on right-hand needle and knit it —1 st inc'd

m marker

MC main color

mm millimeter(s)

M1 (increase) with left needle tip, lift the strand between the last stitch worked and the first stitch on the left needle from front to back, then knit the lifted loop through the back to twist it

M1L (increase with left slant) with left needle tip, lift the strand between the last stitch worked and the first stitch on the left needle from front to back, then knit the lifted loop through the back to twist it

M1P (increase purlwise) with left needle tip, lift the strand between the last stitch worked and the first stitch on the left needle from front to back, then purl the lifted loop through the back to twist it

M1R (increase with right slant) with left needle tip, lift the strand between the last stitch worked and the first stitch on the left needle from back to front, then knit the lifted loop through the front to twist it

oz ounce

p purl

p2tog purl 2 stitches together (decrease)

patt(s) pattern(s)

pm place marker

rem remain(s); remaining

rep repeat(s); repeating

RLI (right lifted increase) pick up the right leg of the stitch below the next stitch on left-hand needle and knit it —1 st inc'd

rm remove marker

rnd(s) round(s)

RS right side —the "public" or outside of your work

sk2po slip stitch knitwise, k2tog, pass slipped st over st just knit

sl slip

sm slip marker

ssk slip 2 stitches one-at-time knitwise, then return them to left needle and knit them together through back loop

ssp slip 2 stitches one-at-time knitwise, then return slipped stitches to left needle and purl 2 together through back loop

sssk slip 3 stitches one-at-time knitwise, then return them to left needle and knit them together through back loop

st(s) stitch(es)

St st Stockinette stitch

tbl through back loop

tog together

w&t wrap and turn (short-row, see Glossary)

WS wrong side —the "private" or inside of your work

wyb with yarn in back

wyf with yarn in front

yd yard(s)

yo yarnover

* repeat starting point

( ) alternate measurements and/or instructions

[ ] work instructions as a group a specified number of times; metric measurements

glossary

CAST-ONS
Old Norwegian Cast-On

This method is set up the same as the long-tail method **(Fig. 1)**.

Use your right hand to bring the needle toward you and under both thumb strands, then swing the tip of the needle toward you again and down into the loop on your thumb, then swing the needle up and away from you, around the outside and over top of the first finger strand, catching the nearest finger strand **(Fig. 2)**.

Bring the needle back down through the thumb loop **(Fig. 3)** and to the front, turning your thumb slightly to make room for the needle to pass through. Pull your thumb out of the thumb loop **(Fig. 4)**, then pull the two strands to snug the stitch on the needle.

Reposition your hand and repeat from Fig. 2 for each additional stitch.

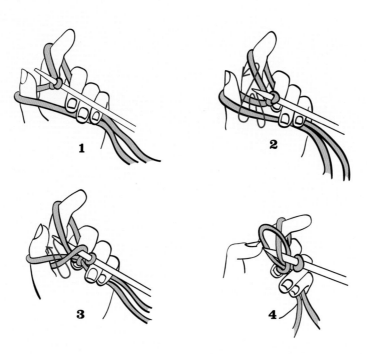

Long-Tail Cast-On

1 | Leaving a long tail (about 1-2" [2.5-5 cm] for each stitch to be cast on), make a slipknot and place on right needle. Place thumb and index finger of left hand between yarn ends so that working yarn is around index finger and tail end is around thumb. Secure ends with your other fingers and hold palm upward, making a V of yarn **(Fig. 1)**.

2 | Bring needle up through loop on thumb, grab first strand around index finger with needle **(Fig. 2)**.

3 | Go back down through loop on thumb **(Fig. 3)**.

4 | Drop loop off thumb and, placing thumb back in V configuration, tighten resulting stitch on needle **(Fig. 4)**.

Turkish Cast-On

This technique lets you work stitches outward in both directions from the cast-on edge.

1 | Hold two needles parallel to each other. Leaving a 4" (10 cm) tail hanging to the front between the two needles, wrap the yarn around both needles from back to front half the number of times as desired sts (4 wraps shown here for 8 sts total), then bring the yarn forward between the needles **(Fig. 1)**.

2 | Use a 3rd needle to knit across the loops on the top needle, keeping the 3rd needle on top of both the other needles when knitting the first stitch **(Fig. 2)**.

3 | With the right side facing, rotate the two cast-on needles like the hand of a clock so that the bottom needle is on the top **(Fig. 3)**.

4 | Knit across the loops on the new top needle **(Fig. 4)**. Your round is now established.

1

2

3

4

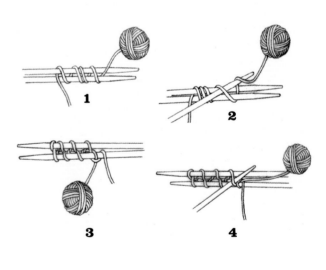

1

2

3

4

Judy's Magic Cast-On

This cast-on technique lets you work stitches outward in both directions from the cast-on edge.

1 | Leaving a 10" (25 cm) tail, drape the yarn over one needle, then hold a 2nd needle parallel to and below the first, and on top of the yarn tail **(Fig. 1)**.

2 | Bring the tail to the back and the ball yarn to the front, then place the thumb and index finger of your left hand between the 2 strands so that the tail is over your index finger and the ball yarn is over your thumb **(Fig. 2)**. This forms the first st on the top needle.

3 | Continue to hold the 2 needles parallel and loop the finger yarn over the lower needle by bringing the lower needle over the top of the finger yarn, then bringing the finger yarn up from below the lower needle, over the top of this needle, then to the back between the 2 needles **(Fig. 3)**.

4 | Point the needles downward, bring the bottom needle past the thumb yarn, then bring the thumb yarn to the front between the 2 needles and over the top needle **(Fig. 4)**.

5 | Repeat Steps 3 and 4 until you have the desired number of sts on each needle **(Fig. 5)**.

6 | Remove both yarn ends from your left hand, twist the 2 strands around each other to secure the last st, rotate the needles like the hands of a clock so that the bottom needle is now on top and both strands of yarn are at the needle tip. If you're using DPNs, work with a 3rd needle; if using magic loop, pull out the loop; knit half of the stitches from the top needle **(Fig. 7)**.

Begin working in rounds.

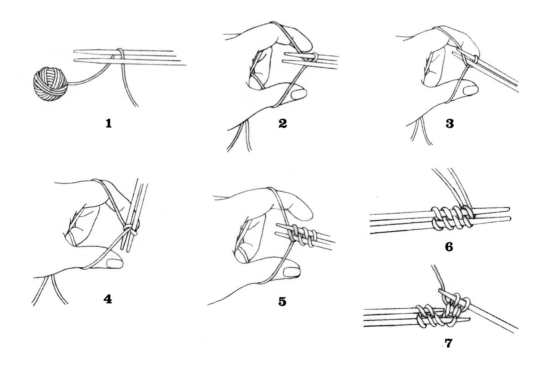

BIND-OFFS

Jeny's Surprisingly Stretchy Bind-Off

This flexible bind-off technique works well at the cuff of a sock.

To "Collar" a Knit Stitch: Bring working yarn from back to front over needle in the opposite direction of a normal yo **(Fig. 1)**, knit the next st, then lift the yo over the top of the knitted stitch and off the needle **(Fig. 2)**.

To "Collar" a Purl Stitch: Bring working yarn from front to back over needle as for a normal yo **(Fig. 3)**, purl the next st, then lift the yo over the top of the purled st and off the needle **(Fig. 4)**.

To begin, collar each of the first 2 sts, working in patt. Then pass the first collared st over the 2nd and off the right needle—1 st is bound off.

*Collar the next st in patt **(Fig. 5)**, then pass the previous st over the collared st and off the needle **(Fig. 6)**.

Repeat from * until 1 st remains on the right needle. Cut the yarn, leaving a 6" (15 cm) tail, then pull on the loop of the last st until the tail comes free.

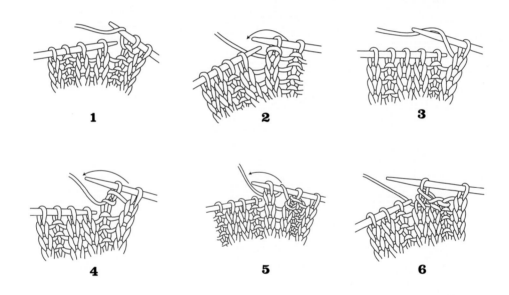

SEAMING

Kitchener Stitch

Set up your work so that the sts are divided evenly across two needles. Cut the yarn tail, leaving about four times the width of the sts to be joined, and thread onto a yarn needle. Hold needles parallel, with needle tips pointing to the right.

1 | Bring threaded needle through first st on front needle as if to purl, and pull the yarn through (**Fig. 1**).

2 | Bring threaded needle through first stitch on back needle as if to knit and pull yarn through. (**Fig. 2**).

3 | Bring threaded needle through first st on front needle as if to knit and slip this stitch off needle, pulling yarn through. Bring threaded needle through next st on front needle as if to purl and leave st on needle (**Fig. 3**).

4 | Bring threaded needle through first st on back needle as if to purl and slip this stitch off needle, pulling yarn through. Bring needle through next st on back needle as if to knit and leave st on needle (**Fig. 4**).

5 | Repeat Steps 3 and 4 until 1 st remains on each needle, adjusting the tension to match the rest of the knitting as you go. To finish, bring yarn needle through the final st on front needle as if to knit and slip this st off the needle. Then bring yarn needle through the final st on back needle as if to purl and slip this st off the needle.

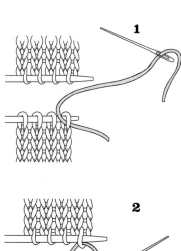

1

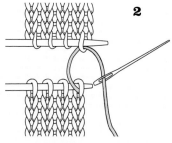

2

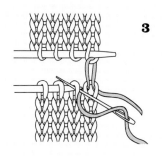

3

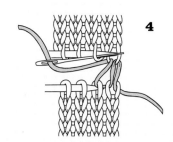

4

SHORT-ROWS
German Short-rows—
Create Double Stitch (DS)

1 | Work to the turning point and turn the work.

2 | If it's not already there, bring the yarn to the front, and slip the next stitch purlwise. If you're facing a purl side, the yarn will already be in front; if you're facing a knit side, you'll need to bring the yarn to the front.

3 | Bring the working yarn to the back over the right needle and pull upward so that both legs of the st below the slipped st are pulled up onto the needle, creating what appears to be an odd-looking double stitch.

4 | If the following row is a purl row, bring the working yarn to the front again between the needles; if the following row is a knit row, the yarn is already at the back in position.

The stitch appears doubled because both legs are around the front of the needle, making it very easy to identify; on a subsequent row/rnd, work into both legs of the double stitch to close up the gap created by the turn.

Wrap & Turn Short-rows (w&t)

Short-rows (Knit Side): Work to turning point, slip next st purlwise **(Fig. 1)**, bring the yarn to the front, then slip the same st back to the left needle **(Fig. 2)**, turn the work around and bring the yarn in position for the next st—1 st has been wrapped.

Working wrapped stitches (Knit Side): When you come to a wrapped st on a knit row, hide the wrap by working it together with the wrapped st as follows: Insert right needle tip under the wrap from the front **(Fig. 3)**, then into the st on the needle, and work the st and its wrap together as a single st.

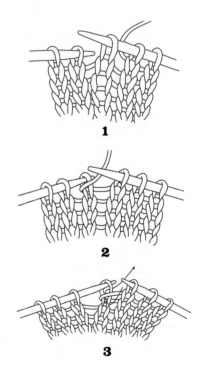

1

2

3

Wrap & Turn Short-rows (w&t)
(continued)

Short-rows (Purl Side): Work to the turning point, slip the next st purlwise to the right needle, bring the yarn to the back of the work **(Fig. 4)**, return the slipped st to the left needle, bring the yarn to the front between the needles **(Fig. 5)**, turn the work around and bring the yarn in position for the next st—1 st has been wrapped.

Working wrapped stitches (Purl Side): When you come to a wrapped st on a knit row, hide the wrap by working it together with the wrapped st as follows: use the tip of the right needle to pick up the wrap from the back, place it on the left needle **(Fig. 6)**, then purl it together with the wrapped st.

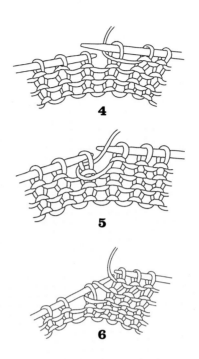

PICK UP & KNIT

Although there are a number of ways to pick up and knit stitches along the gusset (or other) edges, this is the best method for socks.

Pick Up Both Loops

For a sturdy join, pick up the gusset sts through both halves of the edge sts. *Insert the needle under both legs of the selvedge st **(Fig. 1)**, wrap the yarn around the needle as if to knit **(Fig. 2)**, and pull a loop through. Repeat from * for the desired number of sts **(Fig. 3)**.

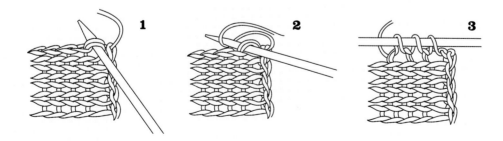